With love and
all best wishes
To our dear friends
and neighbors
Who just missed
Meeting the author

Ruth von Behr

8/13/94

Ghosts in Residence

h. a. von BEHR

Published by
North Country Books, Inc.
Utica, New York

Copyright © 1986
by
H. A. von Behr

ISBN 0-932052-48-7

First Edition

Library of Congress Number Cataloging-in-Publication Data
Von Behr, H. A. (Hans A.), 1902-
Ghosts in residence.

Bibliography: p.
1. Ghosts. I. Title.
BF1461.V66   1986   133.1   86-12539
ISBN 0-932052-48-7

CONTENTS

1   The Old Chase Place   1
The spirit of a Quaker maiden, who lived on the hillside, hovers over a 200 year old farmhouse.

2   The Guide's Warning   24
A guide's warning catches up with house guests.

3   The Grogan Place   44
A 200 year old Quaker farm haunted by an Irish ghost.

4   The Night of the Hunt Ball   52
Riderless horse takes Master to the Hunt Ball.

5   Caroline   61
A beautiful young bride, whose body was strangely preserved in an iron casket on a Chatham Centre farm.

6   The Patriot   70
Patriotic spirits march through Kinderhook during a perilous moment in World War II.

7   Widow Mary   76
Ghosts at the Livingston Manor House.

8   The Dog Collar   83
A message from a faithful hunting dog.

9   The Golden Watch   88
Grandfather's watch came 50 years late.

10   Spooks at the Manor House   93
A royal prince meets a ghost at a country manor house.

11   Castle Bronner   98
      Demons haunt an ancient castle.

12   The Guardian Angel   108
      *Do spirits from another world sometimes
      guide us?*

13   The Rope Bed   116
      A gentle poltergeist in the guest room.

14   The Bright Light   121
      An unexplained phenomenon at the hillside.

15   The Black Thing   126
      *A demon dislodges two consecutive tenants
      from an old village residence.*

16   Merwin's Tombstone   133
      "Ichabod Crane" of Kinderhook.

17   The Butler   139
      *The ghost of a suicidal butler haunts a
      country house.*

18   Good Night   146
      A poltergeist at the home of the in-laws.

19   The Chair Factory   151
      *Shaker ghosts haunt the home of a young
      Scottish couple.*

20   Apple Blossoms   169
      Survival of an ancient spell.

21   The Seer   174
      *Visions of the past are unveiled by a gifted
      psychic.*

*Photographs taken by the author except those
supporting material of the contributors.*

For Ruth

Patsy

FOREWORD

When it comes to understanding the dead, there is something unusual about the Hudson Valley; so many ghost stories have come out of this region. Some have become a part of our national lore such as Washington Irving's retelling of the legends about Rip Van Winkle and Sleepy Hollow. Most, however, have remained in the Valley where they have been retold from generation to generation. I can understand their continuing popularity. When I was a child my parents read to me these stories, and in recent years I have speculated that such dramatic accounts have had a formative influence on what I have found meaningful in a career devoted to the history and art of the Hudson Valley.

There are a great number of stories known and countless more unrecorded. In the early 1940s Prof. Louis Jones' students, in his course on folklore at what in now SUNY at Albany, collected ghost stories from their hometown people throughout New York State. They came up with more than four hundred local stories, most of them from a small area of the state, primarily the Hudson Valley and secondarily from the Mohawk and Schoharie Valleys.

Why so many and why these valleys? I have a hypothesis. These valleys are the longest settled rural places in New York. They were settled by the Dutch and Germans who may have some traditions of ghost stories of their own, but I think what is more relevant, these valleys were later settled by another people, the English, who found the indigenous culture uncomfortably alien and thus inscrutable. Travel accounts of the seventeenth and eighteenth centuries remark on the "odd" customs of the Dutch and Germans and, significantly, on the ambivalent attitude they had toward outsiders.

Strangeness and unfriendliness are the ingredients that play in the mind and call for explanation which in a vernacular culture can be most readily answered by recounting strange events with accompanying folk explanations. If these accounts are appealing or plausible they become elaborated as stories.

And if there is a fear of others, those stories should reflect things that are fearful and nothing is more fearful than death.

Most of the folk tales of the Hudson Valley, and ghost stories are a genre of folk tales, have been passed down by English speaking people, of whom Washington Irving was the greatest story teller. His stories, roughly based on local traditions, played on the differentness of the Dutch. They became established in the local culture as widely accepted explanations for the unexplainable or the different.

Stories are also invented anew, as you will see in the following chapters, by the reoccurrence of inexplicable phenomena. These are first person accounts of actual incidents. Some later on become elaborated by others, who, not having the immediate experience to convince them of its veracity, add to the story to give it greater appeal and thus conviction, just as gossip can be truth elaborated into falsehood in anticipation that the falsehood will sound more truthful than the truth. But the original incident, told by a witness, is the most powerful account and that is what we have here.

Despite our empirical and skeptical age, things happen to many people which just can't be explained by normal perception. Perhaps, as Louis Jones had speculated, science has given us so many explanations for the miraculous in recent years, that we have come to believe that what has been unbelievable will often prove to be real. From his survey it is evident that ghost stories, and apparently the belief in ghosts, are alive and well in our time. Judging by the content of the present book, the occurrence of ghostly phenomena may even be expanding.

Ghosts, as we know them from Louis Jones' survey, have an interesting variety of attributes, some surprising. The most popular stories have to do with buried treasure and the vanishing hitchhiker.

In fact the latter story in its many variations is the most popular of all. In these stories ghosts appear in one of three forms: lifelike, as a reanimated corpse; in a spectral form such as a light; or a misty figure. There are twice as many male ghosts as female (not counting all those vanishing hitchhikers who are female), and about ten percent are children.

More ghosts are associated with farmers and farm families than any other occupation, which is logical as most stories are from rural areas and that is the predominant livelihood. There is a fair number of murder and other disreputable characters and, perhaps surprisingly, clergy. There are animal ghosts too, mostly dogs.

According to these stories, ghosts usually have clear purposes in mind to motivate their appearance. About a third have died violently, mostly by murder, others by accident and suicide. As a result they have unfinished business to attend to. Some are there to warn or inform the living, or to punish and protest, or guard and protect. Some just want to re-engage in their former lifetime trade. A few seem to get pleasure out of reenacting their deaths. A common theme seems to be their discontent with the circumstances of their death which they return to correct. Ghosts engage in just about every imaginable type of activity except procreation and child birth. Certainly these acts of creating life are the opposite of how ghosts come to be, that is, through extinguishing life, but there may be a more deepseated ambivalence between sexuality and death than meets the eye.

The most common activities are pulling the bedsheets off people or just plain walking. About 10 percent actually speak to the living and a third make some sort of noise (steps, groaning, door closing). The one thing that all ghosts have in common, besides being the spirit of the dead, is the ability to vanish.

Surprisingly most ghosts are rather indifferent to the living (58%), others are even benevolent (29%), while only 13% are malevolent and of these almost none cause death to the living, and if they do, it is with cause against a particular person. This doesn't leave any justification for the living to fear ghosts.

One of the most frequently asked questions is, "Do you believe in ghosts?" I think the question is irrelevant; it says more about the asker than the asked. It is like the fellow who asked J. P. Morgan how much his yacht was. "If you need to ask, you can't afford it." If you have to ask if someone believes, then you haven't had a ghost experience and wouldn't understand. I haven't had the privilege, so to speak, so I don't know what to think. It does strike me as rather curious that there are several major religions and a lot more minor religions all prospering quite well on about the same level of verification of the supernatural as contained in ghost stories. Converts to the latter are mighty thin compared to the former. Perhaps it has something to do with a more promising hereafter. I suppose if Mark Twain was to put his mind to the subject he would advise ghosts to take inspiration from the promises of preachers.

One of the most interesting aspects of this subject is not the ghosts but rather the people who do and don't encounter ghosts, or should I say, those whom ghosts find receptive to their appearance. Hans von Behr is just such a person. Many of the chapters of this book are accounts in which he was a principal as well as observer. This book is as much about Hans as it is by him. And it should be, as he is a marvelous person, a sprightly, engaging chap who creates good company for his many friends who all enjoy being with him and his equally appealing wife, Ruth. That spirit of hospitality does appear to extend further than meets the eye as you will read in the story of "The Old Chase Place." I can also tell of another example of this to which I was a witness a month ago while we were sitting on their porch enjoying the end of the day.

Out of the corner of my eye I saw a partridge (ruffed grouse), of which the woods around the farm had always had a good supply, quietly and cautiously hopping out of the woods, across the lawn and under the spruce tree in front of the porch, its head cocked to one side and then the other, listening to our conversation. The more we talked the closer it came. When I softly remarked on its presence and our conversation slowed, it began to hop away. So we returned to our animated conversation and this bird hopped up onto the porch, slowly walked toward Hans, hopped onto the chaise lounge next to him and looked us over. As we stopped talking to look, it began to move away, so we started up again and it became more content. It was as if the partridge wanted to join in the company, finding the conversation pleasant. About then the rain that had been threatening all day started to fall in a steady downpour partially drowning out our conversation.

With that the partridge hopped down under the tree and slowly walked across the lawn into the woods as cautiously as it had come.

I had never witnessed a wild bird relate to people in such a human manner. Hans then told how this partridge, which he had named Patsy, had first come around the house earlier in the year when they had first come up for the summer weekends and how, week by week it had become more emboldened to join them each day on the porch during the happy hour, to the point where Patsy would hop up on Hans' wrist. He had to find a glove to wear as her claws dug into his skin as she held her balance. When they came up to the farm each weekend she was waiting and flew around the car in apparent joy to see them again.

What are we to make of this quite extraordinary relationship between Hans, who each year had looked forward to hunting the elusive wild game bird in those woods, and his new found friend? Was it a plea for him not to hunt again (it worked; he hasn't picked up his new shotgun since he bought it last year) or is there something more to this relationship? Throughout the chapters of this book you will notice how this incident is paralleled by others.

If Hans is unusual enough in his experiences he is also unusual in his ability to relate these experiences, both in writing and in the telling. Hans writes exactly as he speaks so when I read these chapters I "hear" his voice as if he were before me. It is the uncanny gift of the true raconteur. I don't personally know anyone whose presence is so convincingly invoked by reading his writing though I am sure others have had such an experience.

Now it is time to enjoy these accounts for yourself. They follow on a long line of tales on the supernatural, most of which have come out of Columbia County for centuries. Washington Irving's *Legend of Sleepy Hollow* derives from people and events in and around the nearby village of Kinderhook. Louis Jones' *Things That Go Bump in the Night* contains other memorable Columbia County stories. Most of these stories have been told and retold through generations until the original incident, if there was one, that prompted its origin has been lost. The special quality of Hans von Behr's accounts is that they are first person witness to events inexplicable and supernatural. We are present at the creation of stories which will become folk legends in the twenty-first century.

Roderic H. Blackburn, PhD
Albany Institute of History and Art

Further reading:

Louis C. Jones
Spooks of the Valley. Houghton Mifflin, Boston, 1947.

Things That Go Bump in the Night. Hill and Wang, New York. 1959.

"The Ghosts of New York: An Analytical Study", *Journal of American Folklore*, October 1944.

Carl Carmer
The Screaming Ghost and Other Stories. New York, 1946.

Marion Lowndes
Ghosts that Still Walk: Real Ghosts of America. New York, 1941.

CHAPTER 1

The Old Chase Place

It was a drab and chilly March day when I signed the contract of sale to take possession of my 102-acre farm. Old Willoughby Van Alstyne, my agent, had driven me and my dog up to the place for a final inspection. Winter had been slow in departing and, here and there, small remnants of snow still clung to the north side of the stone fences. When we got back to Willoughby's place, a large farm in the Hudson Valley that had been in his family for 300 years, we settled down in the office from which he managed his dairy farm and conducted a small real estate business. I sat down on a swivel chair in front of his roll-top desk and signed my name to the purchase agreement; my handsome English setter at my feet thumping his tail on the floor in approval of the transaction. It was really he who wanted this piece of farmland even more than I did.

Willoughby's wife had prepared a hot dinner of chicken and dumplings, which we ate with great gusto after the long day in the cold and muddy farm country.

It was too late to get a train back to New York, so I stayed overnight in a large, chilly guest room that was

1

furnished with lovely family antiques, including an ancient mahogany four-poster bed covered with a handsome quilt. I slept well this first night as a farm owner. The price seemed low enough, but I still had some doubts about the wisdom of my investment. Little did I know I had struck a bargain, a strange bargain - with fringe benefits.

My photo studio in New York kept me busy, but I was eager to get back to my new country place as soon as the spring weather set in and the muddy lanes became more passable for my small Willys car. I lost no time in getting to my new home in the hills.

I was soon convinced I had found the right place, an old Colonial central hall farmhouse with a hundred acres of fields and weeds in the foothills of the Berkshires. The gray clapboard house on a hillside overlooked undulating farmlands and woods and, on a clear day, it had a beautiful view extending 60 or 70 miles to the west over the Hudson Valley to the skyline of the majestic Catskill mountains. The land that belonged to the farm was far from good farm land. To me and my dog it seemed sheer paradise, though it was referred to, somewhat in jest, by my neighbors as a "good for nothing" farm. This did not lessen my love for it.

On our first walk across my new property my dog flushed a covey of partridges, and soon after raised a cackling cock pheasant down in the swamp. The farm was quite isolated and could only be reached by a climbing, dead-end, woodland road. It was hidden from neighboring farms. In fact, it was so far off the "beaten track" that I had difficulty when I went there for the first time on my own. I found myself driving through a maze of backwoods dirt roads before I could locate my hillside paradise.

Adding to this confusion was the fact that there had been a number of short-term previous owners, among them some recent immigrants who had never become well-known to the local people. I didn't get much help with directions until I mentioned the owners dating back 100 years - the Chase family. That name rang a bell at once. Life moves slowly in these hills, it would seem. Perhaps there was more to it, for I became aware of a questioning look in people's faces when I introduced myself as the new owner of the Chase place. I brushed it aside as merely rural awkwardness and shyness toward newcomers, only to learn bit by bit there was something mysterious about my farm. I began to wonder if there was more than one reason the purchase price had been quite low.

The house itself was very run-down. The previous owners had left in some haste almost a year before. It had remained empty and forlorn in the midst of weeds surrounded by six 80-foot elm trees. The porch sagged badly and tangled chicken wire was loosely attached to parts of the white fence railing, giving away the fact that this spacious old porch had obviously been used as a chicken coop. The cellar, which could be entered from the downward slope of the house, had been used to house cows ever since the barn had burned down years ago, and the smell of rotten cow manure was still apparent. Walls and floors were grimy and in a state of disintegration. The inside alone had probably discouraged most other prospective buyers. There was a broken cast-iron stove in the kitchen, and a hand pump that after much priming produced water from a very deep hand dug well. The rest of the "plumbing" was a three-seater outhouse about 60 feet to the north of the house. It actually had wallpaper as a luxurious feature, although its door swung loose from rusty hinges. Everything needed repair - everything and everywhere, and soon.

In spite of all this, my dog and I were happy to have a roof over our heads and to be in this great countryside.

There was water, and I could do simple cooking on my newly-purchased kerosene range; but most of all we had peace and quiet. We were happy living in simple style in the glory of the rolling hills of the Berkshires. However, I was soon to learn that the deficiencies of the manor house were not the only reason for the low bargain price.

Before the trees had leafed out I had seen a tiny cottage on the other side of my lower hayfield. Walking up to the place one day I saw a small, gnome-like white-haired man with a scrubby white beard. He was busily digging in his garden, but he looked up when he saw my setter dashing ahead of me. Putting down his hoe he strolled over to the garden gate, whereby I introduced myself as his new neighbor.

"I am John Van Steen," he said as we shook hands, "glad to meet you. Glad to see someone once in awhile, though I don't mind living here all by myself. I have good company here with the dog and cat, and my horse and cow over there in the pasture behind the old barn. They are all my pets and we are a happy family here."

John, an immigrant from Holland, had retired to this tiny cottage after many years working as a tailor in Brooklyn. He seemed to be a jolly little fellow with a foxy, much wrinkled face, and we soon became good neighbors. A competent gardener he was; always glad to give me advice and help with my horticulture problems. A week or two after our meeting he came over to my place, his pet white horse drawing a small farm wagon, and he plowed a potato patch for me.

We strolled over to his narrow, slanting porch where he offered me a rickety chair and brought out a glass of tasty homemade elderberry wine. After lighting his pipe and petting my dog, he looked at me in the same questioning way as some of the other local people.

"How do you like the old Chase place? Having any trouble, eh?"

"None in the least," I smiled. "Why should I have trouble?"

"Well," - and he hesitated for minute -, "it's a strange place all right. The last owners couldn't take it any longer, and they moved away in a great hurry. They say it's haunted - spooks, you know. They had had it."

I laughed heartily.

"I don't believe in such nonsense. It's a nice quiet spot and I like it. I'll let you know when I see a ghost, but my guess is you'll have a long wait. Besides, I have a good, alert dog and a double-barreled shotgun. Any spook that comes up our way will get a rough reception."

He knocked out his pipe on the front porch.

"Well, I hope you will come over for a visit to my disreputable place," I said in parting, and headed down the dirt road. To take a short-cut, I climbed over a stone fence to my side of the land and crossed the fields toward my haunted house. The place must have some character, some personality, I thought, but spooks and ghosts were out of the question as far as I was concerned, casting off the idea as utter nonsense.

Old houses - and one as neglected as my pride and joy - certainly are apt to have a strange effect on people, especially city people. But I didn't wish to identify myself with that group. There are lots of sounds, strange sounds - window shutters rattling and, sometimes, banging against the side of the house in the wind; squirrels that hop around in the attic rolling nuts and acorns around.

There were chimney swifts in the old unused flues; harmless little birds. They flutter up and down in old chimneys, especially at night when they come and go hunting for mosquitoes and moths in the air. They are good useful birds, although their wings touching the walls of the flues can make an eerie sound. The rustle of leaves in trees, bird songs, and even rain sounds, are soothing to the ear. They are healthy sounds, far more palatable than the never ceasing roar of the city with its fire engines, police sirens, garbage grinding, dirty streets and summer heat waves.

Returning to my haunted house, I took a folding chair out to the "lawn," better described as a hay lot, and lit a pipe as my setter stretched out on the grass, tired from the long stroll through the fields. My new status, that of the owner of a haunted house, amused me. Nothing in my background could bring me to accept the idea of haunts and ghosts. I had been a research chemist after I left college, a true realist. My father had been a professor of physics. There had been no room in my upbringing for such nonsense. Now it began to dawn on me why I had been able to buy the place at such a reasonable price. It had, as we say, "a bad reputation." This didn't bother me, and I slept well, refreshed by the cool night air that blew in the open windows. The next morning I set about the endless tasks before me to get the place into shape and order. Since rural electrification did not bring electric power and light to our countryside for years to come, lighting and cooking were done with kerosene. But this turned out to be very pleasant and quite acceptable when you get used to it. It took much hard work on my part, money and patience to improve or merely maintain an almost 200-year-old farmhouse.

One beautiful summer morning in July as I was having coffee out on the lawn after breakfast, my dog rose and let out an alert, though not unfriendly, bark. Turning in the direction of some damson trees that surrounded the overgrown garden patch in the back of the lawn, I saw a woman emerge from the cover of dense bushes. She seemed a pleasant looking woman about 40 or 50 years of age, who might have looked older than her age. She was wearing a faded print dress and a bonnet-shaped straw hat and was carrying a basket containing empty kitchen pots. She approached me rather timidly.

"I'm your neighbor from over the back of the hill and I wonder if you would allow me to pick some huckleberries. They are just ripe and there are lots of them in your upper pasture."

"Well, of course you can. Take as many as you want. No one else picks them here," I said.

Before she started on her way to the fields she took time out for a pleasant conversation about the fine summer weather, the farms and the people of the neighborhood. She was a farmer's wife who owned a small place about a mile east. She had walked all the way along an abandoned road that leads through my woods. Before she set out for picking she asked the same question as my Dutch neighbor.

"Aren't you scared to be in this old house all alone? It's such a lonesome place. I wouldn't like it here."

"I suppose that's just why I'm here. I love being alone in this peaceful, silent country," I replied. But this didn't end the conversation or change the subject.

"Well, what about nighttime? Don't you hear any ghosts?" she inquired with a whimsical smile. "They say they do carry on here - the last people had to get away. Couldn't take it any longer. They even shot at the spooks before they gave up the place. Let me show you where the shot was fired, right back there in your summer kitchen. You can still see the shotgun pellets that punctured the pantry door."

I laughed, but I was curious enough to have her lead me to the back, called the summer kitchen, and there, clear and obvious, was the pattern of a shotgun blast right through the upper panel of the pantry door, as she had said. I had never become aware of it until now. I hadn't noticed - but there it was. I even picked out a lead pellet with a knife.

"I'll be darned," I said. "It seems they should have used silver pellets. That's the only way to shoot at a ghost. Nothing else will do."

After this enlightenment, I assured her there had been no ghosts since I had moved in, had never seen nor heard one, and that I didn't sit around waiting for one either. So we parted company. She set out with her basket of rattling pots to fill them with lush, sweet huckleberries. I finished my cold coffee, smoked my after breakfast pipe in peace and quiet with Dash, my dog, at my feet - thinking over the new tale of my haunted environment.

All this neighborly concern had aroused my curiosity, and it seemed to call for some research into local history, which might throw some light on my house's "past" and the matter of its "bad reputation."

My efforts in this direction soon produced some interesting information. I learned that over a hundred years before it had been a Quaker boarding school. There had been additional buildings, now completely gone with barely a few foundation marks in evidence. The school had been conducted by a Cornelius Thurston Chase. The entire vicinity had been a Friends Settlement and their meeting house, built in 1777, was located less than a mile west of my boundary lines. Still standing and used as a farm grainery, it was in a much more rundown condition than my house. My search also revealed that a young teacher, Phineas Gurley, who was later to become Abraham Lincoln's minister, and who sat at the bedside of the dying president and preached the funeral sermon, had once taught there. I also found at the New York City library a book of poems of Mary Mehitable Chase, published by Ticknor & Fields, Longfellow's publishers, in 1854. In addition to Mary's poems, the book also contained many long letters written by her to her friends. They described in great detail the life in her Quaker household, written in her sensitive and poetic style. It told much about the people who came to visit there. It also described Christmas celebrations and told of nearby neighbors, their African women servants (Friends had no slaves), her observations of nature, farm animals and pets, and climatic conditions. From her writing it was obvious that this young Quaker girl, who at the age of 33 died from tuberculosis, or consumption as it was called then, had loved her home very much. Her last wish had been to be buried on the nearby hillside slope under her favorite apple tree, the old arm tree, so called because of its extraordinary branch formation. I located the forgotten and overgrown burial plot only a few hundred yards west of my house. There I found the sunken plot fenced in stone, about 18 x 25 feet, and covered by myrtle which had spread over almost a third of an acre all around. Could it be that this kindly, romantic Quaker girl would be haunting her old home? Perhaps, and there could also be a reason.

It seemed understandable that she had resented the people who had owned this place shortly before I took over because they had let it become run down and, in so doing, had desecrated her beloved homestead. I had been told that they even shot robins for food as they were very poor and at times hungry. Was it her determined haunting that had eventually driven them away in haste and fear? Could her haunting have stopped suddenly, to give me, the new owner, a chance to put her home back into shape, saving it from further abuse and giving it an honorable and orderly status? Perhaps her observations of my plans and slow progress had calmed her, and I had perhaps received her seal of approval. So went my meditations as I tried endlessly to undo the mystery of my new house. Were my assumptions right? Would there be no more haunting and no more ghosts? Time would tell.

As my house became more and more orderly and attractive, it was natural that I would want to share my little paradise in the hills with some of my good friends from the city. There soon were weekend guests; young

The house at night.

*A simple Vermont marble slab marks the grave of
Mary M. Chase, facing west in Quaker tradition.
Early Quakers did not use any markers for their graves.*

The Old Chase Place when I first came upon it.

*Lead pellets remained in pattern of
shotgun blast in upper panel of pantry door.*

John van Steen and his pet white horse.

The Quaker Meeting House, built in 1777,
now restored and used as a family home.

and full of joie de vivre. There were young professionals
and artists, their pretty wives, and some beautiful fashion models. All enjoyed this great country, so much in
contrast to their exciting city lives. Wine, women and
song, much gaiety, and often long night sessions with
conversations over scotch and soda took place over fre-
quent weekends, and a new atmosphere, quite unlike
Quaker tradition, had taken over. After all, we were all
young and carefree.

Soon this change in tempo produced a reaction. One
beautiful fashion model and her husband had some
frightening experiences. During the middle of the night
they both saw a pale and ghostly female figure in white
staring at them from the foot of their bed. Later, while
everyone was asleep, including my watchful dog, they
heard footsteps in the hallway. Another guest refused to
go up to her bedroom alone, even during the day. We
tempted her with a $100 reward, but she firmly turned
down the offer.

A few weeks later, two young New York girls heard an
eerie scream in their room. No one else heard the sound,
including the dog. They were so frightened that they left
the house in the middle of the night, and we found them
wrapped in blankets sleeping on the lawn the next morning. They never came back for another visit.

A beautiful ballet dancer who had occupied the largest
of my three small guest rooms, the one in which Mary
Chase had died about a hundred years before, reported
with trembling voice that a female figure in a long white
swishing garment had passed her bedside. A feeling of a
cold chill on this balmy July night had accompanied this
manifestation as it dissolved moving slowly through a
closed door. We calmed the ballerina over her morning
coffee, but I was left wondering, with some envy, about
these strange experiences. Perhaps my friends were
psychic and I was not so gifted.

The following year I spent the summer in Europe, and gave the key to the house to a poor young Russian artist who wanted to do some landscape painting there. He stayed only one week, frantically begging his friends to come and fetch him so that he could go back to New York. When his rescuers arrived they found him sitting with his bag and baggage next to the mailbox, half a mile down the hill - along the roadside. He had to get away from the place where he had some frightening experiences. He reported an apparition of an old sea captain, standing in the door frame of his bedroom, staring at him and scaring the poor artist into a paralyzing fright. He never came back to finish his landscapes.

Although I was not unsympathetic, I could only reject all this as fantastic nonsense. I myself had never heard a sound nor seen swishing, floating figures, had never heard any footsteps or screams at night, nor did I have the honor of a visit from the old sea captain. One of the Chase's neighbors, I later learned, had been a sea captain. I also knew that Mary's mother had come from a seafaring family in Nantucket.

Why was I spared or even deprived of all these mystic goings on? Perhaps my time had not come and I felt left out. Was it that the shy Quaker girl approved of me, but not always of my friends - rather a presumptuous conclusion since I was certainly not in any way more Quaker-like than my good friends. However, I loved my house and tried my best to bring it back to its original charm and dignity.

Time went by and it was years before my turn came. There were lovely summers and I enjoyed my days up there, together with my faithful dog. One evening on a clear and balmy night I was sitting in a comfortable lawn chair under the tall 100-year-old elms. Above me was a clear sky full of bright, sparkling stars. I had brought my portable radio outdoors and was listening to a concert broadcast from nearby Tanglewood. It was a great place to enjoy a musical performance, all alone, away from the crowded concert audience. My mind had wandered to an incident that had happened earlier in the season. An old car had driven up to my place one day. From it emerged a plain looking, middle-aged couple with a flock of children. They introduced themselves as descendants of the Chase family and asked if I would show them the old family homestead. I had been very glad to oblige, and had shown them all around the place. Upon their departure, I had presented them with a bushel basket of fresh vegetables that had grown in my garden in great abundance. I had far more than I could use for my own needs, so it had not been a deprivation on my part. They seemed to be simple people and, much to my disappointment, they had nothing specific to tell me about their ancestors and their claim to the Chase lineage. It had left some doubt in my mind as to the authenticity of their story. To my surprise they appeared a second time a few weeks later to find me somewhat reluctant to be the same good host. And then, only a few weeks later, they came a third time. As I saw the car in the distance turning into my road I took to the woods with my dog, pretending that I was not at home, so they drove away.

Later that same afternoon a raging thunderstorm lashed up from the west. It poured buckets, and lightning cracked down in all directions, hitting one of my elms. It tore tree bark and white elm wood splinters, throwing them more than a hundred feet. It was a very close strike to my house, but the tall elm had absorbed the blow instead, acting as a naturally protecting lightning rod. As the storm lessened, heading east into the Berkshires, I opened the kitchen door to let in the fresh, moist air. A small bird fluttered into the house, soaking wet, trying to find a safe place to dry its feathers. I picked it up. It was exhausted and I placed it in an empty bushel basket. There it sat for a long time, seemingly grateful for its rescue from the storm. When it had stopped raining, and the bird seemed dry enough, I took the bird in the basket out to the lawn and he soon flew away.

Was there, perhaps, any link between my inhospitable behavior during the third visit of the Chase's to the frightening storm and the visit of the small bird? I dismissed the thought and accepted it as a natural coincidence, while I was sitting under the lovely clear summer sky, listening to the great music from Tanglewood.

And then it happened. From the direction of Mary Chase's grave on the western hillside, I saw the strangest phenomenon that I have ever experienced. A white, shapeless, luminous form emerged, about 10 or 20 feet across in the irregular form of a gigantic amoeba. It rose slowly, moving toward me, gradually rising over the small barn toward the lawn.

The dog had risen and was cautiously stalking the strange floating ectoplasm. His hackles had risen as I had never seen before. He moved as though pointing a game bird, with his tail straight, but the fur on his back was upright, showing his fear and apprehension. I too had gotten up and was walking slowly toward the strange, white floating object. It rose higher, and then changed its course slowly toward the north, disappearing behind the tree crowns, and finally moved completely out of my vision behind the structure of the house. It is hard to tell how long it lasted . . . perhaps 15 to 20 minutes. When the phenomenon had disappeared, the dog and I returned to the lawn chair and, somewhat perplexed, I wondered what it was all about and what it could possibly be. I ruled out the possibility that it could be a cloud - there were none in the sky. And it was much too solid a mass for swamp gas. It had a form and it was not at all hazy. But now it was gone and I was left wondering. The concert music had stopped and it was near midnight.

The next morning, glancing through Mary Chase's book, I came across the date of her birth - August 12, 1823. Today was August 13, another lovely summer day at Hillside Farm, as the place was called by the Chase family in her time. I felt that I finally had met up with the unexplained, that there were things I could not brush away as fantasy. It had finally happened to me.

Hearing my story, my more sophisticated friends in the country - and city - felt that I had fallen off my rocker. This old research chemist and confirmed skeptic now claimed to have seen an apparition at his lonely house in the Berkshires. Although not a frightening experience, it had finally convinced me that things take place in this world that cannot always be explained. I knew it had happened and I tried to find a reason for its happening, and if it bore any relationship to the people who had lived in my house a hundred years ago - a kind and intellectual family of Friends including a daughter Mary who had dearly loved the house and the countryside.

Is she still perhaps drawn to it from another world, a world of the unknown? Did she want to communicate with me and give me a message? Who knows?

That episode was followed by many years of ghostly silence. I married and carried my bride over the threshold, much to the amusement of the carpenters and masons who were working on the house at the time - replastering walls, repairing woodwork and building a new chimney. One of the workmen, standing by during our arrival, showed his obvious approval of the mistress of the house by this laconic comment, "pretty good pickings."

The house soon showed rapid improvement due to my bride's feminine touches, her good taste and excellent talent for interior decorating. We slowly gathered inexpensive early American antiques at local auctions which identified well with the old homestead. We raised our young son, and the child and wife stayed there through summer and fall seasons - often alone for days with only our faithful setter for companionship and protection. Though I had told her about the reputation of our manor house, there was not a single incident to frighten her. Perhaps the spirits had given their full approval of this new domesticity and felt no reason to interfere. There was only one occurrence during that period of years, and it was rather comical.

It seems derogatory comments about our house may be taken in "good spirit" by us, but not necessarily by our invisible tenants. One of our house guests, a young man of about 30, had expressed in a rather boisterous manner that our house was old and shaky, and our restoration efforts had been foolish and a bad investment besides. We both ignored the unflattering criticism. Bedding down for the night, our house guest rejected the guest room we selected and had chosen to sleep on the sofa in our dining room where it was warmer.

That night he was suddenly and rudely awakened by a splash of water thrown in his face. There was no possible source of water - such as perhaps a leaky pipe - for he slept on the south side of the house, and all the plumbing was in the northern section. The nearest source of water was at least 30 feet away from his resting place. It seemed a real poltergeist prank; more amusing than frightening.

Aside from this one capricious incident, the spirit world that had been around us remained totally quiet for years. This lasted until our son grew into manhood. Our place was popular with his friends, and he brought them home frequently as house guests. All was well until one summer a beautiful, bright, but wild, untamed and "way out" young girl struck his fancy. She promptly took the lead and in a manner that disturbed and concerned us . . . and finally, also our son. During this uneasy summer things began to happen . . . again.

One night, while the two youngsters were out, my wife

and I heard footsteps in our son's room, and finally a thumping down the stairs. At first we thought the young people had come home, but upon investigation we found their rooms empty and no one else in the house. They did not return until hours later, so we have no explanation for it.

Another time our unruly house guest reported in a rather unconcerned manner about a strange apparition during the night in her room; the room where Mary Chase had died. She described it as a hazy figure in white, sitting at the bottom of her bed, and finally moving away with the sound of a rustling gown. This incident, however, did not unnerve her in the least and it was soon forgotten.

Weeks later after the risky romance had ended, and all the household was sleeping soundly, we were once again awakened. This time by a rattle at the old batten door that leads from the master bedroom to our son's room. It seemed like an obvious effort to open the thumb latch door handle, causing loud metallic clicks. It was about two in the morning when we called to our son to stop the nonsense and go back to bed. He replied gingerly from his bed, "Maw, I am in bed. I heard it too."

Later we heard footsteps down the hall and thumping on the stairs. But now that the romantic tension had ceased, summer days and summer nights were peaceful again. Perhaps the spirit of Mary Chase had calmed down with us after she had successfully registered her objection to the hazardous teenage romance.

There is only one more incident, of recent date, to report. Our son had some young friends, a brother and a sister, who lived with their parents in the restored Quaker meeting house about a mile from our place. They were a devout Catholic family. Late one evening, while the two young neighbors were visiting with us, we were all enjoying a hot cup of tea in the kitchen. Our attention was suddenly drawn to the top of the oven where a five-pound heavy 12-inch cast iron frying pan suddenly started to shake, soon to rise about two or three inches and then thump back on the oven top. We were all very much taken aback by this. The event soon became known and was carried by local gossip in our village. We wondered if Mary Chase, the Quaker girl, took offense to our Catholic friends since in bygone days there was great tension between the two religious groups. My wife, who had recently learned that ghosts like to be talked to when they make themselves known, gave Mary a good lecture. She told her that she had no reason to object to our Catholic friends. After all, they had saved her old meeting house from complete deterioration by having it restored to become their home. She must have taken this talk to heart. There have been no more strange happenings since that time.

The one-time skeptic is no more. On the other hand, I don't believe one can sit in a so-called haunted house waiting for something to happen. I do believe, however, that departed spirits who maintain an interest in our world may go into action in their own way, of their own volition and in their own time. Drawn to the past, to a place or people, they may try to take a hand in our lives; sometimes destructively, more often protectively. At times they startle or frighten us, but I wonder if this could be just another way of trying to guide us. If we're not listening, their actions may remain completely concealed from us, and, we may never know that the other world exists.

Our house is blessedly haunted. We feel convinced that a guardian spirit hovers over it from time to time, and we have listened and become conscious of it. So, guided through the years, we have found a happy house amid the unspoiled rural charm of the Berkshire foothills.

CHAPTER 2

The Guide's Warning

Before we turn our back, at least temporarily, on The Old Chase Place and look at the haunted homes of our friends and neighbors, and other mystic phenomena, I want to tell one more "ghost in residence" happening that took place at our old farmhouse not too long after I bought it.

The place had slowly begun to get into shape and become habitable. The most essential of all improvements had been the plumbing. Water was now brought into the house from an old 45-foot-deep well by a gasoline powered pump. At last there was a kitchen sink with hot and cold water, a bathroom and even an outdoor shower bath. Furniture had arrived: beds, tables, chests of drawers, all "second best" Montgomery Ward Early American reproductions. This had helped to transform this empty shell of a rundown house into a modest, pleasant home. The only guest that I had invited before, while it was in its rough state, was Max, a tall six-foot friend who, when so inclined, had given a hand with my never-ending tasks. The time had come, and I was eager and ready to invite house guests.

Among the first to venture to come for a weekend was a young couple, Don and Jane Flowers. Don, a slim, handsome fellow with classic features like a Greek Apollo, was a very successful cartoonist. He produced a syndicated weekly comic strip called "The Modest Maidens," showing two shapely beauties going through all kinds of subtle adventures. His wife was the most beautiful brunette I have ever met. Her outstanding, refreshing charm, captured by some of my studio portraits, had promptly established her as a top-ranking Powers model.

They had promised to drive up Friday afternoon. I had given clear instructions and had drawn a map showing every landmark, every turn, especially for the critical last three miles from the village to my house. Max and I had already arrived at the farm the previous evening. It was a balmy midsummer's day, and we sat on the lawn anticipating the arrival of our guests in the late afternoon. We enjoyed an extended cocktail hour watching the sun set in pink and red glory behind the bluish-gray silhouette of the Catskill Mountain range. Finally, we went inside the house, lit up the kerosene lamps and prepared our gourmet meal of hamburgers and mashed potatoes.

"Max," I said, "those kids will have a rough time finding their way along those winding chipmunk trails in the dark. My fine road map will not be of much help to them after sunset. Well, I had warned them about this."

Don, a chronic procrastinator, always did his best work when under the pressure of his weekly deadline. He would dawdle, play jazz records, smoke cigarettes, and sip Cuba Libres - and finally get to his drawing board, working until all hours of the night. That most probably had been the case this time; sleeping late into the morning, and then finally they had started on the trip in their dashing sports car.

Max nodded in agreement to my suppositions and we returned to our chairs on the lawn, looking up through the heavy foliage of the towering elms under the star-spangled sky.

I was right. Don and Jane arrived in the Village past 10 P.M. There was not a light shining in the Village houses. Country people go to roost early. There was no one to ask for directions and my detailed road map had become almost useless in the darkness. They drove out of the Village, in the wrong direction, when they came to a brightly lit building, the Grange Hall, where they pulled up with great relief. Several old ladies were chatting in their rocking chairs on the porch. The chic young couple, happy to have found some sign of life, marched up to the porch.

"What can we do for you folks?" a gray-haired old lady inquired.

"We are looking for a friend of ours, Hans von Behr, who bought a farmhouse hereabouts in the hills. Perhaps you can direct us."

"Never heard of him - nobody buys any farms around here these days."

"Never seen him in church," was the comment of another old character.

"Maybe they don't believe in no church."

The commotion had brought out a crowd, curious and eager to be of help.

Don showed the map, but that was no help.

"What's the name of the place," someone asked, "Who had it before?"

One fellow came up with a bright suggestion: "Reckon it's the place where the old policeman died."

"What did he die from?" a bright eyed lady chimed in.

"Oh, forget it," someone snapped back, "their friends would not live in that little old shack."

"How about the Murphy place - been empty for years."

"Nobody lives there now," a young fellow explained. "Been over there last week hunting for woodchucks - nobody lives there now."

Jane shivered even though it was a balmy summer night. "Let's go back home."

"Back home - 150 miles?"

Suddenly Don remembered that I had once told him about the old Quakers that lived in my house about 100 years ago. He turned to a young fellow wearing a baseball cap.

"It's a very old house - Quakers lived there at one time." That hit a note. The young fellow, beer can in his hand, perked up.

"Now you're talking, Mister. I think I know the place. It's the old Chase place, up there at the end of the Seven Bridges Road. Yeah, that's where it is. There was a family living there for a few years, but they packed up and run."

"Why?" Jane asked.

"Well, Ma'am, they were scared out of their wits there by a ghost. Yes, Ma'am, a ghost. They had it and they couldn't take it any longer. I wouldn't want to spend a night there either. But if you want me to, folks, I will be glad to take you there. It's a short drive. Just follow my car, it's sittin' there across the road."

"Thank you so much. That's awfully good of you," Don replied with a deep sigh of relief.

"No trouble, folks. Just follow me, but don't ask me to go into that house."

Don and Jane hopped into their convertible while the guide got his old Dodge started. It had a broken muffler and made a great deal of noise. He whisked along at some speed - first back to the Village, then he made a sharp turn left onto a bumpy country road - another sharp turn right onto the winding Seven Bridges Road. There was no trouble following the guide. The sound of the broken muffler heralded his whereabouts. After another sharp turn and then driving up a short grade he stopped and got out of his car.

"There it is folks - just follow the stretch of this uphill run. I won't take you up there, if you don't mind. I'd rather not." Before he turned his car he gave Don and Jane a strange, questioning look.

"Do you *really* want to go up there? Well, good luck - you may need it!" and the helpful guide roared off, leaving them alone.

It was another half-mile drive up the narrow road, encroached from both sides by tall trees, and the dimly lit house did not come into view until they were right in front of it. Here Max and I were waiting, swinging a barn lantern to lead our guests to the house.

Gingerly they followed us. They had never been in a simple farmhouse like mine. We offered our guests a much-welcomed drink.

"Everything will look a lot more cheerful in the morning," we assured them as they gulped their scotch and soda and reported the harrowing experience they'd had in finding the place. They were still tense from their journey, and the dimly lit house did not put them at ease. We had to keep them company until the last ice cubes had melted and dawn was almost ready to break over the ridge in the east. Taking one kerosene lamp with us, we carried their luggage to the best guest room and bade them good morrow - at last.

Late, very late, in the morning our guests descended and joined us for a long delayed breakfast on the porch. It was a beautiful summer day. Birds were everywhere and the old Chase place glowed in its summer glory, as if trying to make up for the nightmarish arrival our guests had experienced.

It could not have turned into a happier weekend, though Don and Jane remained timid about going alone into some of the different rooms, especially to their guest room upstairs. But they loved the house and the beautiful country around it. Not only did they repeat their visit, but they felt inspired and considered buying a country home of their own. This, however, turned out to be an ill-fated venture. A few weeks later almost in tears, Jane told me how they had found a nice old farmhouse across the Hudson. When they drove up again the following weekend to close the deal, they rummaged in the attic of their potential country paradise, and, to their horror, they found some old faded photographs showing two open coffins displayed on the front porch. Terrified and shaken, they both ran to their car never to look again at country real estate. This misadventure, however, did not discourage their occasional weekending with me.

One time they brought along a date for me - Ilene. A Powers model like Jane; she was just as beautiful and charming. Needless to say, I could not have been more delighted. Ilene seemed much impressed with the farm, though cool to me. Sweet and polite, she kept me at a safe distance and soon it became clear to me that I had failed to be her type. Instead, she turned all her charms on Don. Soon the two were off for a long walk in the woods. Jane was furious, as a perfect summer weekend wilted in the bud.

Birds were singing, a balmy breeze brushed by the sunbathed lawn, but nothing could lift the fog of disenchantment. I tried my best to comfort Jane as she rested her beautiful face, now almost in tears, on my shoulder. "It's all my fault," I consoled her. "I simply failed to play my part. Perhaps I was too over-eager, too solicitous, which may have turned off this lovely creature. I take all the blame. I am sorry."

Jane shook her head. "No, no," she whispered. "I am afraid I should have known better. You did not have a chance."

"Am I so hopeless, so ugly or silly not to be able to interest a pretty girl? Why didn't I have a chance?"

"You didn't," she sobbed. "Promise never to mention it. Perhaps I shouldn't even tell you. But Ilene is very much at ched to a very famous man - that's why. I can't even tell ou his name.

"Really!" I gasped.

Jane nodded. "We should have left her in town."

This at least threw some light on the gloomy atmosphere that had fallen over our weekend. There was more scotch and soda sipping than usual as the sun headed toward the Catskill Mountains. One thought crossed my mind: Mary Chase, our prim and proper house ghost was not going to like all this. Because of her disapproval, some of my other un-Quaker-like guests had received an eerie welcome on previous occasions.

The long summer evening, without our habitual joie de vivre, moved on slowly and bedtime came to our drowsy group earlier than usual. Don and Jane's guest room was adjoining Ilene's. There was a narrow batten door connecting the two places. Followed by my setter Dash, I retired to the master bedroom across the wide center hall. Soon the great silence of a country summer night, with only the leaves in the tall elms rustling in the cool breeze, engulfed the old house on the hillside.

Several hours must have passed when Dash rose from his bearskin rug beside my bed. Something had attracted the attention of the watchful and alert dog. His growl, as he went slowly toward the door, awakened me from a deep sleep. I thought that I too had heard some muffled voices, then a short suppressed shriek came from across the hallway. A squeaking door was opened, a glimmer of light appeared at my doorsill. My guests, carrying a kerosene lamp, were in the hall, descending the stairs. I jumped out of bed, turned on my flashlight and put on my robe. I found my guests in the small dining-living

*The Old Chase Place after it had been
brought back to its original beauty.*

*The 45 foot deep
hand dug well with well sweep.*

*The squeaky old
handpump in the kitchen.*

All hands on deck:
Guests give the old manor house a coat of paint.

Jane Flowers, posing at the studio for a life insurance company advertisement.

Jane Flowers, studio portrait.

room downstairs. The two girls were huddled together on the sofa, shivering and weeping. Don was preparing some fresh scotch and soda in the adjoining kitchen. Puzzled by the nocturnal activity, I joined my distraught guests.

"We are going home." Jane looked up at me, her beautiful features woeful and teary. "It was terrible, ghastly - Ilene saw it too, this ghostly thing. It entered her room through the closed door. We have never been so frightened in our lives. I hate this place. We must go home right now."

Don, bringing in some drinks from the kitchen, looked at me with a gloomy, accusing expression, his hands shaking as he put down the glasses. "Yes, yes," he addressed me. "The girls are right, and so was the kind fellow from the grange who guided us here on our first visit. Your house *is* haunted!"

"Yes - she came through the closed door from the hall. We were already awakened by some light footsteps on the stairs, then in the hall. At first we thought it was you and the dog. But no, a rush of cold air enveloped our room. And then this ghostly white figure came right through the closed door, stood at the foot of the bed staring at us, though we could not see a face - only the long grayish-white cape and the head covered by the whitish bonnet."

"We were petrified," Jane chimed in, "I could hardly breathe. I wanted to scream but I couldn't. Then the thing floated over to Don's side of the bed and lingered, perhaps a minute or two."

"What happened next? Where did the spook go? Did it disappear?" I asked.

"Not so soon," Don explained. "She turned toward the door to Ilene's room. Then we heard a shriek."

"The thing came to my room. A sudden frigid chill had awakened me," Ilene sobbed, drying her tears. "It gazed at me, sitting on the side of my bed. I was paralyzed. I

tried to scream, but I just stared at it. Then after awhile
it faded away into nothing. Then I heard Don and Jane
move around. They knocked on my door and came to see
if I was all right. We all were shaken and shivering. We
were cold and could not say much. Then we put on our
robes and came downstairs. We don't ever want to enter
those guest rooms again. We want to go home - now!"

"Well," I said, "I am really terribly sorry. Yet, it is
hard to believe. Here I am, mostly alone in my little old
house and not once have I had the honor - let's call it the
dubious honor - of meeting the ghost. But, let's be sensi-
ble. You cannot leave now in the middle of the night.
Look at Dash there, peacefully sleeping at our feet under
the table. He's not scared."

I suggested making some strong hot tea to make us all
feel better. By the time the first pink rays of the rising
sun entered through the east window, my guests had
somewhat recovered from the shock of their harrowing
experience, and I persuaded them, sleepy and exhausted
as they were, to return to their rooms, which now basked
cheerfully in the morning sun. Dash, as their gallant pro-
tector, was to stay with them at their bedside.

It was late in the morning when we all gathered at the
breakfast table. There my guests admitted that the three
of them had all huddled together in the large double bed.
"Let's not fall asleep; we may never wake up again,"
Ilene had whispered to Jane before they gave themselves
up to the arms of Morpheus for a few hours of sound
sleep that extended late into the morning. Dash had finally awakened them by jumping on the already crowded
fourposter bed.

The lovely summer day tried to make up for the terrifying experience of the night before. They stayed on until
late in the afternoon. A happier mood settled over our
quartet by the time they got on their way carrying bou-
quets of field daisies and buttercups in their arms.

I was left alone now pondering over the events of the weekend, analyzing the activity of the discarnate entity. As in previous and also later occurrences, I felt certain that we were dealing with the spirit of Mary Chase, drawn to her old homestead which she dearly loved. This, for example, is expressed in her poem, *My Native Hills*, shown in the following pages. Perhaps she maintained a desire to participate in our world. I always believed that Mary was no evil spirit, never wanted to frighten us. She merely wished to communicate with us. Not being psychic, I have often felt left out, ignored by the disembodied intelligences that have sporadically hovered over our house.

Perhaps a brief postscript will be in order to clear up one of the turns in the story. It was months later when the four of us spent a pleasant evening together in town, ending with dinner at Luchow's, a German restaurant. As we were leaving, walking though the crowded aisles of this enormous restaurant, Ilene stopped at a table where a small party was seated. "Hi," she called to a distinguished, diminutive man, who looked perhaps like a middle-aged lawyer or Wall Street broker. "Hi, Charlie, I want you to meet my friends." As we shook hands with the cordial, dapper gentleman, she smiled; "This is my friend, Charlie Chaplin." Ilene had to make the introduction a second time. I would never have recognized the great comedian, so different from the world-wide image he had created of himself. Now at least we had come face-to-face with the great performer, Ilene's boyfriend - my peerless rival.

MY NATIVE HILLS

I stand once more upon the hills,—
  The great hills, wide and high!
And childhood's feeling through me thrills,—
  'I'm nearer to the sky.'
The dark pines deck them with a crown,
  The snows a mantel lend,
And many a cottage warm and brown
  Upon their lap they tend.

The glorious hills! I speak their name
  With a quickening pulse of pride,
My cheek hath a flush, my eye a flame,
  As I press their mighty side.
I feel that whate'er is theirs of light,
  And beauty and love, is mine;
For I was born, on a summer's morn,
  Within their sacred shrine.

The first green fields mine eyes beheld
  Lay wide upon their breast,—
The first sweet flowers my weak hands held
  Were stolen from their crest.
God bless the hills—my native hills—
  The 'proud strength' he has given!
And still the feeling through me thrills,—
  'I'm very near to Heaven.'

THE FALLEN OAK

I've been among the winter woods, where winds
    are raging high,
And wildly drifting snow descends in masses
    from the sky;
Down in the glen where sunken graves were
    deftly hid, they said,
In which the Mohawks solemnly interred their
    honored dead.
With timid tread and fearful foot, I crossed the
    narrow marsh,
Where the branches of the alder-tree and horn-
    beam grated harsh;
And on the farther side I stood, and a feeling,
    almost awe,
Kept back awhile my very breath, at the solemn
    scene I saw:
Prone on the moss, beside the swamp, there lay
    a giant oak,
Whose mighty bulk had fallen late beneath the
    woodman's stroke;
Its rugged head full well I knew, that once right
    proudly there,
A Saul among the forest trees, rose up so high
    in air,—
I knew it, when a little child, my father carried me
Upon his stalwart shoulder forth, the blessed
    woods to see.

Oft have I stood in darkened rooms, beside the
    bed of death,
And seen the coldly glazing eye, and heard the
    gurgling breath;

And a lesser feeling like to it, came o'er me as I
    stood
Beside the prostrate trunk of that old monarch of
    the wood;
I could have wept right bitterly, but tears would
    not restore
The uncrowned sovereign to his throne, his sceptre
    give once more.

I knelt upon the snowy moss, to count the
    circling rings,
That round the oak tree's iron heart each coming
    season brings:
Three hundred years recorded well upon that
    mighty girth,
Had passed with all their changes by since that
    old tree had birth.
Then in the distant ages back I noiseless seemed
    to go,
The sky above was clearly blue, and green the
    earth below:
Old storm-defying pines upreared their black
    masts in the sun,
And heavy hemlocks swept the moss, with foliage
    dense and dun;
I saw the lithe arms of the ash out o'er the
    morass reach,
And interlace with shining boughs of birch and
    water beech.

Bright flowers were nodding gaily there, and
    Summer breezes round
Woke up, amid the pine's green harps, a soft and
    pleasant sound;
The red deer slept their noontide sleep, the panther
    on the tree
Closed up his fiery eyes, nor watched his destined
    prey to see;
The falcon drooped among the boughs, the singing
    birds were mute,
The brown bear slumbered careless near the
    bramble's purple fruit;
A stout oak heaved its arms on high, topped
    with a leafy crown,
And as in royal pride and state, upon its peers
    looked down.

A wail rang through the silent wood—a cry of
    woe and wrath,
And the tread of many feet was heard, along the
    grassy path;
The startled deer dashed swiftly by, the panther
    climbed aloft,
The brown bear closer coiled himself among the
    mosses soft.
Down the green slope a long train came, and in
    their midst they bore
A burthen wrapt in shining skins, with plumes
    and flowers spread o'er.
Loud rang the death wail, for they brought their
    warrior king to sleep
Forever in that lonely spot, where lay the shadows
    deep:

They hollowed out with reverent care, between
    the stones, a space,
And sat him upright in his grave, and toward
    the east his face;
And laid his arrows by his side, his strong bow
    in his hand,
That he might chase the flying deer when in the
    spirit land:
Then heaped the warm, dry mould above his
    lately heaving breast,
And with a last wild cry turned back, and left
    him to his rest.

The vision faded,—once again, among the leafless
    wood,
I saw the white storm drifting wild through cold,
    blank solitude;
The birchen saplings bent their heads before the
    rushing gale,
The young pines swayed, and little twigs came
    rattling down like hail:
I stood up in the howling storm and said—O
    fallen tree!
The relic of a buried world dost thou appear
    to me!
Sole witness of that shadowy past, whose story
    none can tell,
Nor guess the wild and strange events that in
    those haunts befell!
In thy prime, a century old thou stood'st
    when winds of June
Wafted o'er 'Unknown River' bold Hudson's
    staunch 'Half Moon';

Thou saw'st thy mates around thee fall, and the
full blaze of day
Into thy secret woodland haunts find its unwelcome
way;
Around thee rose the grove once more, and gentle
creatures came
To dwell with thee, where timid flowers shrank
from the sun's bright flame;
Before the axe had found thee out, strong, full of
years wert thou,
For every Summer brought green leaves to
wreathe thy hoary brow.

But down the white storm thicker came, and on
my thoughts intent,
I slowly turned my steps away, and up the
wood-path went;
And felt that 'twas a fitting shroud, heaven's
wildly whirling snow,
For that old king who ruled these shades,
three hundred years ago.

CHAPTER 3

The Grogan Place

The first time I saw the Grogan place was the day I was being shown the farm which I now own. The realtor, Willoughby Van Alstyne, had taken me from farm to farm across the county. Late in the afternoon we had come to "The Old Chase Place" up on the hillside at the end of a dead-end uphill road. I had fallen for it the moment I saw it.

On our way back to his office we soon turned into a dirt road which runs along a small brook. Winding in snake-like fashion along the valley, the brook crosses the road seven times. This one-mile lane is marked on the county road map as the "Seven Bridges Road." We had crossed two of the seven small bridges when we ran into a stretch of deep mud that proved too much for Willoughby's old black sedan. We skidded to the right, wheels spinning in the soft mire. The car stopped. With rear wheels hopelessly sunk in the muck, we soon realized that we could not get the vehicle going again without some help. But all this had not changed Willoughby's paternal good humor.

"You wanted a place far away from anybody. Well, I showed it to you and this mud bath is the price you'll have to pay for living in this isolated neck of the woods. But I will get you out of here, don't worry. Just below here is a farm. I know the fellows who run it. They will give us a hand. Come on, let's walk."

Only a few hundred feet ahead we saw the farm, barn-red painted cow shed and silo, and the white clapboard house just across the road. Jim Grogan, a sturdy fellow in his forties, wearing blue overalls, was standing at the barn door almost as though he had expected us.

"Hi, Jim," Willoughby hailed him. "This here fellow may become a neighbor of yours - so we hope. But right now we are stuck in the mud up here on the hill. Could you give us a hand?"

"Heard all the motor racing and wheel spinning - let's take a look," Jim replied in an amiable way as he joined us on the short walk back to the disabled vehicle.

"We'll need the team to get this thing out of that mud puddle - need horses to get your bus on the road again. I'll get them - just wait here." Jim waved his hand as he headed back to the barn. It didn't take long for him to return with the sturdy team; a black gelding and a white mare. The powerful horses pulled our disabled car out of the mud without much effort and, before long, we were back at the Van Alstyne home where, after a tasty meal, we prepared the binder for the purchase of "The Old Chase Place."

Jim and I became good neighbors. The Grogan farm always appealed to me. Nestled in a valley of fields and pastures, edged by wood lots at the near horizon, it looked snug and peaceful. Jim and his brother Dan owned a small heard of Holstein cows, the handsome team of horses, some pigs and fowl . . . almost all that was needed at that time to make a good, self-sustaining living on a farm. It had been in the Grogan family for a couple of generations. In the fall, when harvesting was finished, Jim enjoyed going hunting with me while his brother Dan took care of the farm chores. He admired the performance of my dog in the field as he had never before hunted with a well-trained hunting dog. We followed eagerly as the setter pointed pheasants among the rustling cornstalks and elusive partridges here and there in the alder and aspen patches along the brook. Jim was sporting an exceptionally fine Parker shotgun.

"A rich man's gun you are carrying. You can't miss with that one," I said to him. Jim laughed at the remark about a rich man's gun. Who could have imagined then that this would be the instrument of grim tragedy?

Returning to his house after many hours of trampling through the fields and swamps Jim often asked me in for a cold beer. The old farmhouse always impressed me. The unusual steep roof covering the storey and a half clapboard frame house made it look different from the general architecture of old New England/New York State farmhouses. It had the style of a house in the Dutch countryside. The great heavy, hand-hewn beams and the exceptional wide pine boards covering floors and ceilings obviously made from the original virgin timber of the region, proved that it must have been built early in the 18th century by the first settlers. Like wise old sages, old houses reveal so much fascinating lore. Years later, thumbing through local historical material, I learned some more about the venerable old house.

The first settlers started by living in simple log cabins, gradually and laboriously turning the mighty forest into fields and pastures. When sawmills became available in nearby settlements to cut the great pine logs into boards and beams, houses like this were built.

Records reveal that a William Brown owned the place in the latter part of the 18th century. The story goes that he was awakened one night by some squealing and

Dash is looking birdy, and the hunter hoping for a point.

The Grogan Farmhouse.

The Grogan Farm

rattling noises in his barnyard. He grabbed his musket to investigate, but his spouse told him not to go out into the pitch dark night. He waited until she had fallen asleep again and then tip-toed out of the house into the darkness. There he saw two glowing eyes near the pigpen. He raised the gun and aimed between the eyes of the intruder. He fired and went back to bed. The next morning he found a dead bear with a half eaten porker in his mighty claws. Such superb marksmanship in the pitch dark night is almost too hard to believe. According to local records this was the last bear to be killed in the vicinity.

At the turn of the century he sold the place to William Coffin, a Quaker from Nantucket. He had been a sea captain and at the end of his last voyage he had traded a rich cargo of sealskins in New York that brought a tidy profit. Ready to leave the sea and settle down on a farm, he had joined his Quaker friends in the Rayville settlement (then known as Greenbrook or Quakertown) and bought the place which his family farmed for generations. In 1880, the Grogan family took over. Jim and Dan, the two bachelor brothers, became the last of this family to farm the 150-acre place.

The small dairy farm provided a pleasant and independent way of life in the country. Except for the daily calling of the milk truck, the brothers did not see many people. An occasional trip to town in their old Chevy coupe was about their only contact with the outside world. But they seemed happy and content with their isolated way of life. I drove by occasionally on weekends, waved to them or stopped for a brief chat. During the winter, tending to my studio in New York, I heard little of what was happening in the country. One day, reading the weekly local newspaper, I saw a short notice covering the death of Jim's brother Dan.

When I drove by again in spring, passing the small

dairy herd munching their cuds in the lush pasture on the hillside, Jim seemed to be avoiding my company. At times I got a glance of him working around the barn. He seemed strangely shy and depressed; his neighborly friendliness had disappeared, and I did not wish to force my company on him in his obvious state of deep mourning. People in the Village told me that Jim had become a changed man since his brother's death. Rumors were that he had seen his brother's ghost; that it was haunting him wherever he went, following him around in the barn as he milked the cows and fed the horses. The ghostly apparition did not even give him peace in the house. His brother's ghost was said to follow him wherever he went. Perhaps he was begging him to join him.

The summer went by and I returned to the city. There later I learned that Jim had died - a suicide. Tortured by loneliness, grief and the restless haunting of his brother's ghost, there in the room to the right as you enter the house, Jim had shot himself in the head with that Parker shotgun - the one I had called the "rich man's gun."

Soon the farm was sold. The new owners never lived a day in the old house; the ghostly atmosphere of the place scared them away. In a short while the farm was for sale again.

It has changed hands several times since and has ceased to be an operating farm. Today it is the summer residence of Mr. and Mrs. A. K. Cheney, a family from New Jersey, who cherish and enjoy the old house with the steep roof in its pastoral setting. Grogan's ghost has gone to his final rest in a world beyond.

CHAPTER 4

The Night of the Hunt Ball

The weather forecast had been discouraging . . . rain, drizzle, fog for the entire weekend. But we decided to go to the country in spite of the weather. There is always some fixing to be done in an old house like ours, and there are also friends and neighbors to sit down with in front of a cozy fireplace and enjoy each other's company.

We had decided to take the late train and then drive from the station to our place. It happened to be the night of the Hunt Ball, a gala affair held annually in the Fall in an old tavern, a tavern that had served as a coach stop on the Albany Turnpike in the 18th century. The fairly large clapboard building, now owned by one of the club members, had not been occupied for years, but was kept up in good repair. Some of the old timbers were beginning to deteriorate and the small tavern dance floor was considered safe for only a few couples at a time. Tonight was the Ball, and the old building would be all decorated for the festive occasion. It would be attended by the members of the Foxhunt, the men all dressed in "Pink," wearing their scarlet hunting coats, giving the old tavern a nostalgic atmosphere as if the clock had been turned back a century or two. Those who were not riding members, the ladies and guests, would arrive in dinner clothes and, as always, everybody would have a great time at the Ball.

The windshield wiper was clicking away as my wife and I drove the 30 miles from the station to our house. We had chosen to take the back roads to avoid the possible traffic confusion in the Village center caused by those attending the Ball. We were members of the Hunt Club, although not riding to the hounds. Our status was that of "Porch Members." This implied that we sat on our own or our friends' porches, with drinks in our hands, watching the colorful hunt go by; the horsemanship, the crying (baying) of the hounds as they rode over the countryside, chasing the fox. The cunning creature most always outfoxed hounds and hunters, sneaking along pasture fences and hedges and, if necessary, going to ground and safety in the nearest woodchuck hole. All this provided great sport for fox, hounds and hunters alike, and great horsemanship and courage was needed to "ride to the hounds" in a foxhunt.

Perhaps we should have taken an earlier train and attended the party. But this would have meant bringing our evening clothes from the city, getting dressed in a cold and damp house and then driving along muddy roads in our finery. We had decided against making the effort and settled for a quiet, casual weekend at home. There was another reason we had decided not to attend. We would have missed our good friend John presiding over the festivities as Master of the Hunt. It would have been the first Hunt Ball that John was not attending. He had died almost a year ago, and the happy affair just did not seem the same to us without him.

John Carroll had been a great guy, an excellent horse-

man and an enthusiastic foxhunter. He was a tall strong
man, built like the star in a western cowboy movie, with a
ruddy outdoorsman complexion and a witty twinkle in
his brown eyes. His spicy sense of humor, sometimes
shocking, added to his strong individual personality, and
he provided great fun and good company for his circle of
friends. Besides being a sportsman, he was also a highly
esteemed painter, and in strong contrast to his rough
outer shell his paintings were delicate and sensitive, his
romantic style perhaps vaguely reminiscent of the Span-
ish painter, El Greco. He had painted portraits of many
prominent people, making them appear slim and ethe-
real, a style appealing especially to his feminine sitters,
and his work was represented in many galleries and
museums. His graceful, delicate wife, "Pinky," had inspired him and modeled for many of his museum pieces.

Whether outdoors with his horses and hounds, or at
his New York studio, he had enjoyed life to the fullest.
Riding cross-country from his 200-acre farm, he would
occasionally stop for a stirrup-cup at our place, sometimes with a riding companion, but more often alone. He
would come downhill along a stony road and then canter
across open fields, where the Hunt had set up hurdles to
make the sport more challenging to expert horsemen.

I was first introduced to John by a charming redhead
who brought me to his farm. At our arrival we heard
sharp metallic banging and we found John in his small
smithy, hitting hard hammer blows on a red-hot horse-
shoe. He did not even look up and returned our hello
with a mere grunt. We waited around, almost ready to
turn and leave when he put his blacksmith tools aside.

"It's time for a drink," he muttered and took us into
the house. From that time on we became the best of
friends.

Now he was gone. Nevertheless, his frail, yet spirited
widow, still kept the house, the stables and some horses

The Carroll Place.

John Carroll, the painter.

The Hunt.

The tavern, where the Hunt Ball was held. It had served as a Coachstop on the Albany Turnpike in the 18th century.

just as though John were still there.

We were talking about him and the good times we had together as we drove through rain and drizzle along the winding dirt roads. It was almost midnight when we came out from a woody stretch to an open area within a half a mile of our house. We were startled to see several car headlights and what seemed to be people with flickering flashlights moving about in a large pasture. It was an eerie spectacle on this rainy, pitch dark night. Approaching the scene, we stopped to talk to a man about to climb over a fence with a halter and a rope in his hands.

"What's going on here?" I inquired, recognizing one of our farm neighbors.

"We are trying to round up a horse. There is a runaway horse out there and we are trying to halter it here in Roger's pasture. We don't know who it belongs to. It seems to have come from that stony path past your house. We have it cornered here in the field. It's a great night for rounding up runaway horses!"

There wasn't much we could do about helping. Those farm fellows knew what they were doing, and so we drove on to get home and warm ourselves in front of the woodstove and dry up after the chilly, rainy drive.

By the next morning the rain had let up. Curious about the horse roundup I called the farmer we had talked to the night before.

"Well," he said, "we got the horse all right. It's in my barn now. It was John's big, rangy chestnut hunter. It's hard to believe it would have left its fine pasture over at their place where it had all the good timothy to graze on and a dry shelter. And here the fool critter sets out on a five-mile run through the woods, jumping fences and all and coming down that stony trail above your place. The fool critter was heading straight for the Village - might have wanted to go to the Hunt Ball."

I saw the muddy hoof prints on the path right past my

house, and the eerie incident of the night before seemed to verge on the supernatural. What was that horse up to? Had it set out, with an invisible rider in the saddle, to take its master for this midnight ride to the Hunt Ball?

CHAPTER 5

Caroline

Returning from a trip abroad, I was glad to come back to my farmhouse. My good friends and neighbors, Dr. and Mrs. Estabrook, had been instrumental in helping me to find the place and later aiding me with the frustrating task of restoring the 200-year-old homestead.

Only a few years before, they had been through a similar stint putting their old farmhouse into shape and their expert advice had been of immense help to me. As soon as I had unpacked my travel gear and settled down in my house, I set out to call on my neighbors. Dr. Estabrook, with a Ph.D. in Biology, was many years my senior and I respected his scientific mind and his ranging practical knowledge in many fields.

We were sitting in comfortable wing chairs, facing the flickering logs in their fireplace, and surrounded by beautiful family antiques. I had finished my report, and Ann (Mrs. Estabrook) was ready to give me the latest news about our countryside and our mutual friends.

"You missed some big excitement here while you were away. We have a good spook story to tell you."

Nothing could have surprised me more than a "spook story" told by my practical, down-to-earth neighbors. They were firm disbelievers in any form of mystic matters and the good doctor, a realistic scientist, was a most outspoken skeptic.

"You, too," she continued, "may find it hard to believe. But we saw it with our own eyes, as did many others, only a few weeks after you sailed. It happened about a mile from our house at the James Thomas place. There was an old vault on that property - a private family burial plot you might call it. The solid stone structure had given way to the ravages of time, and a large opening at the collapsed stone wall had tempted a local boy to crawl into the crypt and investigate. There he saw two or three wooden coffins rotted away exposing skulls and bones, but there was also one solid iron coffin. It had a glass window, about 6″ x 10″. Removing the dust of ages and looking through the glass window the young fellow saw a beautiful young woman, dressed in a bridal gown and holding a rose in her right hand over her breast. Her features were perfectly preserved as if she were sleeping. Even the rose in her hand seemed as fresh as if it had been plucked yesterday."

"The young fellow chose not to keep his eerie discovery a secret and soon it was talked about by everybody around here. A pilgrimage of curious people set out to see the strange phenomenon - including us."

"Well, of course," the good doctor commented, "a hermetically sealed coffin could preserve a corpse for some time. But the young woman was buried about a hundred years ago. Even if she had been submerged in formaldehyde, which she was not, it would have shown definite deterioration. I admit, it's hard to explain."

Fascinated by this strange phenomenon, we watched the cinders of the fireplace glow dimmer. There was much to tell and my travel report seemed a trifling matter compared with this local event.

Many years passed and much of the captivating detail escaped my mind.

Then recently, December 30, 1976, my good friend, Albert Callan, publisher and editor of the *Chatham Courier* (Chatham, New York), retold the story and has given me his kind permission to reprint it in my book. It could not have been presented by a more expert reporter and writer.

THE VISION IN THE VAULT
A BEAUTIFUL YOUNG BRIDE'S BODY WAS STRANGELY PRESERVED IN AN IRON CASKET FOR 80 YEARS ON A CHATHAM CENTRE FARM

Snow covered a small hillside on Phelps Road, the Town of Chatham, just 40 years ago this week as Trooper J.C. Dwyer of the New York State Police Patrol at Chatham, walked over open fields to a private burial plot on the James Thomas farm.

The trooper had been summoned to keep away the curious after the top of a stone vault had crumbled allowing the public to view the well preserved body of a young girl through a 6 x 10″ glass panel in her coffin.

During the summer of 1936, a young boy discovered that the front of the vault had been smashed in and he entered to gaze upon the face of the young girl, almost lifelike in the metal casket. A baby's bronze coffin and three disintegrated wooden burial boxes were nearby still containing skeletal human remains.

For weeks, there was almost steady night traffic to the Thomas farm as young and old, carrying candles, torches or flashlights, made their way to the old crypt to view the young woman. By autumn the front of the vault had been refaced, but then, when the top of the crypt caved in, the troopers were called.

Trooper Dwyer scoffed at reports, according to the *Chatham Courier* of December 30, 1936 that there had been a grave robbery, saying that the vault had not been rifled, but that the top had merely crumbled, exposing the coffins.

But the curious still came, by the scores, to see what lay in the cell under the wooded knoll. Joel B. Hayes and his family, who lived on the James Thomas farm, had been awakened many nights by trespassers bent on visiting the "Vision in the Vault."

Others came boldly to his door asking information as to the phenomenon - how long had it been on view, what kept it from going to dust like the other bodies there . . . who was she? Mr. Hayes would shrug in response to the inquiries. He hadn't known the lady. All he knew was that the tomb, as it does today, bears the inscription, "Family Vault of Doct. John and James Sutherland - 1842."

Opinions differ as to the first time the vault was usurped. Some say it was about 1905 that someone first broke a lock on the crypt and pried an iron plate from the top of the coffin which had been affixed over the glass pane.

Word went around Chatham and vicinity via the "whisper" route that the long-buried body of a village belle had escaped the ravages of time. But, the vault was then reinforced and would not be entered again until the summer of 1936.

Those who entered the burial place recall wiping away the dust to see the pretty face of a young woman. A rose held in her right hand over her breast was whole. With the discovery had come several legends from the lips of older residents of Chatham.

There was one about an old sea captain who, in the

The Estabrook House, built by a master builder about 1850.

Abandoned Crypt on Phelps Road near Chatham Centre, was erected in 1842 as the family vault of John and James Sutherland. Three times it was violated by ghoulish vandals who reportedly were seeking to remove the coffin of a young woman whose perfect features could be seen through a transparent pane.

early days of the 19th century, had taken his consumptive daughter on an ocean voyage in a vain attempt to save her life. It was said he had brought along the iron coffin so that if she did die, she would not have to be buried at sea. The glass panel was explained by the belief that the captain wished to have a proper land burial when he returned home and that the transparent pane would provide one last look at his beloved daughter.

Another story recalled the death of a young mother whose baby died with her and was buried by her side. Weren't the white clothes on the young girl in the casket her wedding gown and didn't the tiny metal box beside her contain the infant's remains?

With the arrival of Trooper Dwyer at the crypt, Chatham was about to lose its whispering sensation that had gone on for decades. No more would men plot to steal the frail chrysalis, to strip the wedding ring from the hand that held the rose, to place it on public exhibition for a price.

The late Lester Gifford, a Chatham undertaker, was summoned at the request of a distant relative of the Sutherland family. The metal casket containing the remains of the young woman, the tiny reliquary next to her and the stark skeletons of three other persons were removed and given proper interment in the Chatham Centre Cemetery.

Placing all the whispering and misinformation aside, the facts of the "Vision in the Vault" are these. The late Mrs. Aaron Ford Williams of Chatham Centre knew the whole story.

The casket with the glass contained all that was worldly of Mrs. Caroline Sutherland Layton, who had been placed in the metal receptacle on the first anniversary of her marriage.

Caroline, only daughter of Dr. John and Maria Wilbur Sutherland, was born in Chatham Centre and educated at Miss Willard's School in Troy. At the age of 23 she was married in Newark, New York to John Layton who took her to live in Rockland, Illinois.

The wedding bells that rang for Caroline struck disconsolate echoes in many a Chatham swain's heart for she had been the reigning beauty of the town.

Just short of a year later, Caroline died in childbirth at the Illinois home of her husband. A funeral was held there and the body was sent to Chatham for a second ceremony and burial.

Hence the glass window in the sealed coffin of iron - so that Chatham relatives and friends might have a last glimpse of her radiant visage before she was consigned to the ground.

Little did they dream, the loving ones who devised that windowed box of iron, that it would be the cause of so much disturbance many years hence.

It was on the anniversary of her wedding day that Caroline's body arrived in Chatham for her last rites. The year was 1855. Eleven days after Caroline's death, the tiny girl to whom she had given her life also passed away. The baby's body was sealed in iron, too, and sent to Chatham to rest beside her mother in the Sutherland vault.

Caroline was buried in her wedding gown and on the proper finger was a plain band of gold - her wedding ring. That, according to Mrs. Williams, was the only jewelry she wore, as far as anyone was aware.

Yet, over a period of time the Sutherland vault was thrice violated by ghoulish vandals who may have conceived the notion of selling the remains which might have had a definite scientific value.

Since the ancient Egyptians placed their Pharoahs in deep crypts under desert sand, the art of preserving the human form after death has been lost to mankind. Comparatively recent attempts to keep human bodies intact have only been partially successful.

Yet the chemical accident that resulted in the preservation of the beauteous Caroline's form could well have interested embalmers. There were no noticeable signs of any disintegration of her body even after a century of burial.

Mr. Gifford removed the remains on a specially cushioned truck to the cemetery where Caroline was reburied among her mother's kin. During the transfer from the crypt, the undertaker discovered that the bottom of the iron casket had, apparently quite recently, rusted through. The metal box was therefore wrapped in canvas, placed in a rough box and placed under protecting earth away from prying eyes. Her baby girl was buried beside her.

Today, winter winds whip across the fields on Phelps Road sending tiny whirlwinds of snow spinning across the crumbled vault that held Caroline's remains for so many years.

But there are those who will attest that the beautiful young woman was not always a prisoner within the metal box or confined to the brick and steel confines of the old vault.

There are some who claim that on a certain night in June, when the winds are gentle and the stars are soft in the sky, the vision of a young woman in a bridal gown, carrying a white rose, sweeps from the crumbling crypt to walk through the fields near Chatham Centre. Those who have seen her, say she stops frequently to pick daisies and then stops by a stream to pick the petals as if asking "he loves me - he loves me not?" Her nocturnal foray it should be noted is in mid-June, and it could be considered an extreme coincidence that a yellowed parchment in Rockford, Illinois notes that Caroline Sutherland joined hands with John Layton in wedlock on June 13, 1854. But that's another story.

CHAPTER 6

The Patriot
From the *Chatham Courier*, 1979

This is a true ghost story. The time: A cold, blustery night in March, 1942. The place: The handsome brick dwelling on Kinderhook's Broad Street erected in the 18th century by David Van Schaack.

Ten persons had gathered about a crackling fire in the old mansion, which, after being in the Van Schaack family's possession for over a century, was about to be sold.

Flickering flames sent shimmering shadows over the room and the night's silence was broken only by eerie creakings as the wind whistled through the great trees in the yard.

What tales the old house could tell if it could speak!

It was in the mansion on an October evening in 1777 that a group of men rode up on horseback wearing blue army tunics with buff trousers. They were accompanied by three men in scarlet uniforms, but unarmed.

Outside the restless orderlies held pawing horses, while through the open front door went the uniformed men to be welcomed by the host and hostess and their adopted daughter.

The men in blue were American officers under the command of General Phillip who had been directed to march Major General John Burgoyne and his conquered British army of 3,000 by the shortest and most direct route to Massachusetts following their defeat at Saratoga.

Now they were in Kinderhook. General Burgoyne and his two aides had left their troops in a woods not far distant while they accepted an invitation to dine at the Van Schaack mansion. That night camp fires blazed in a brilliant ring around Old Kinderhook.

Within the mansion, fireplaces illuminated the rooms and in the dining hall were stately brackets holding tapered candles, which sent a soft glow over those at the silver-laden tables.

The well prepared meal was a welcome one for both the American and British officers who had been living on meager camp fare for weeks on end.

Toasts were drunk from glasses holding deep, rich claret to "Gentleman Johnny" as Burgoyne was known in the enlisted ranks, and to a distinguished Virginian and commander of the American armies, General George Washington.

Then, without notice, the Van Schaack's daughter, Lydia, arose and lifted her glass to "His Majesty the King and all the Royal family."

At first the Americans gasped at such effrontery while a slight smile stole over the countenances of the British officers. But General Phillip, in a spirit of gallantry, accepted the snub to the Colonial cause and passed it off lightly.

After all, the Van Schaacks had entertained a number of men devoted to the American Revolution. Chief Justice John Jay, Alexander Hamilton, General Philip Schuyler and Chancellor Kent had all dined at this very same table.

Dinner guests at the historic Van Schaack mansion in Kinderhook saw a ghostly figure on the wall during the winter of 1942 that led them to believe the old saying that American patriots do not sleep in their graves when the nation is in peril.

The foxhunt in the field.

Our story returns to that March night 37 years ago. The thoughts of those gathered around the fireplace were not on the American Revolution but the present war. The nation had suffered a cataclysmic blow to the Pacific fleet at Pearl Harbor, while General Douglas MacArthur and his command were making a valiant last stand at Bataan and Corregidor.

It was one of America's darkest moments. Hitler was in command of Fortress Europe and the Wehrmacht was expected to pounce on England. The Japanese were marshalling great forces in the Pacific and rumors ran rampant of possible attacks on America's west coast cities. German submarines were operating off New York City landing saboteurs and agents on the east coast. The conversation at the dinner table was sombre and those present were apprehensive.

After dinner the 10 filtered out of the dining room and settled down before the fireplace where coffee was served.

Then, and without warning, a light breeze seemed to stir through the room as if a window or door had opened suddenly.

One of the guests, a young woman, looked at the expanse of wall above the fireplace and pointed. She was so overcome with fear that she uttered not a word.

Everyone's eyes followed her finger and there, clear and distinct, was the shadowed outline of an American soldier of the Revolution. Slowly, with musket in hand, he seemed to march across the wall and disappear into the darkness.

Awe-stricken, the guests sat silently, trying to account for what they had seen. Was it the spirit of one of the American officers who had been in that same room on an October night in 1777?

Someone recalled the old adage that patriots could not sleep in their grave when the nation was in peril. Were the ghosts of the Revolution marching that night to the side of their beloved America during its moment of anguish?

Yet those who were in the Van Schaack homestead that night will never forget the shadow on the wall. Possibly the patriots did march, for only a year later MacArthur began his offensive toward Japan while a giant arsenal was growing in England for the eventual landings in Normandy.

Who can tell?

CHAPTER 7

The Widow Mary
From the *Chatham Courier*, October 23, 1948

There are said to be many ghosts in Columbia County, Revolutionary soldiers, Indians, young girls, headless horsemen, and various other varieties, but one house, known as "The Widow Mary's place" at Bell's Pond in the town of Livingston and now owned by Mr. and Mrs. E. A. Fitch, has more than its share. It has, or had until Mrs. Fitch got rid of one of them, three spirits who conduct their singular activities after the witching hour.

In 1796, Henry W. Livingston took for his bride, Mary Penn Allen, daughter of Chief Justice Allen of the Pennsylvania Supreme Court. Henry was enchanted with the young lady. She was completely beautiful and charming, and although she had been petted and adored all her life she was not the least bit spoiled. He soon discovered also that she had great capabilities. She could run a large household smoothly and efficiently, and entertain any number of guests without the slightest flurry.

Henry, who had been attached to the American Embassy in France, and had held various posts in Washington, had resided in all parts of the world. Now, he

decided he ought to have a real home, a proper setting
for the beautiful Mary.

He began to think about architects and architecture.
While he was in Italy he had seen several houses designed
by one man. He had liked them all. This, then, was the
person to send for.

The matter of selecting a site came up next. The
house, of course, would be built somewhere on the Livingston lands in southern Columbia County. Henry and
his wife mounted their horses and began a tour of the
manor.

They rode over thousands of acres, through pathless
woods never before penetrated, down hills and through
ravines. One lovely, clear day, as they rode up a steep
incline and across a plateau at the top, both stopped
breathless. They had found their site. They were on a
high hill, directly below lay a small lake of the clearest
water, and the view, Henry estimated, extended for sixty
miles.

Henry's architect came from Italy, and the work
began. Under the watchful eye of the Italian, and of the
owner, who was there every day, the house rose quickly,
so that by the end of the year it was finished.

"It is," said the architect, with a satisfied smile, "the
finest private residence in America." And it was.

Now Henry and Mary began to entertain. All the great
and near great visited them. They gave great balls, and
the house was filled with music and laughter.

Then, suddenly, the music and laughter stopped. In
1810, Henry and Mary went to Europe, but they were
restless, and planning their return home when Henry
became ill and died. Broken-hearted Mary had his body
sealed in a lead casket, and began the slow sorrowful
journey home. A brick tomb was built near the now silent
house and the casket was placed in it.

Mary went back to the house on the hilltop and shut

herself in. She remained there for a long time. Friends
and relatives grew frightened, but eventually her youth
and high spirits came to her rescue. She began to see
people again, and to venture out. Soon she was laughing
as of old, and if her widow's weeds made her look paler it
only added to her charm.

She became the "Widow Mary"; no one called her
anything else. She began to entertain again. She could
speak of Henry again, without tears.

Once again the Hill, as the house was called, became
an international social center. The Marquis de Lafayette
came there, as did Jerome Bonaparte, former king of
Spain, who arrived with a suite of thirty people. When,
after a visit of several days, he was leaving, and the
Widow Mary stood on the steps bidding him goodbye, his
daughter suddenly called for her drawing materials.
Everyone thought it was the view she was sketching, but
those who looked at her pad later discovered it was the
beautiful "Widow Mary."

She had many suitors, of course, for she was still
young and beautiful, besides being fabulously wealthy.
She smiled and charmed them all and then, stroking her
widow's veil between her fingers, sent them away.

She lived a long time after her beloved Henry, not
dying until 1856. The house was then sold by her heirs to
James Bell, but its identity as the Widow Mary's Place
was never lost, and that is how people still refer to it
today, more than a hundred years after her body was laid
in the brick tomb beside that of her husband, and then
the structure sealed for ever and ever.

Oddly enough, it is not the wraiths of the Widow
Mary, or Henry, who wander through the house and flit
around the grounds now, but the ghosts of others who
have much less connection with the house.

When the Widow Mary lived there she was never
alone, for there were temporary guests and there were

Widow Mary's house at Bell's Pond.

permanent guests. One of the latter was a young girl who was with her guardian, a Livingston. She had a suitor of whom the guardian did not approve. Every night he would ride near the house, and the girl watching from her window would signal with a lamp whether it was safe for him to come to the house.

The affair dragged on and on. She would not give up her love, and her guardian would not relinquish his disapproval. Then she died, perhaps of that unexplicable thing that doctors then called "a decline."

Shortly after her death, a villager returning to his home late one night glanced up at the house. It was closed, the Widow Mary being away, but he saw a light flashing back and forth in the girl's window.

He went home and in awed whispers told his wife. She cautioned him not to mention it, people would think he was crazy. But others saw the light. The story of the girl's sad plight was common knowledge and it did not take someone long to say it was her unhappy ghost still trying desperately to signal her lover.

The light has continued until this day, and has been seen by many people. There is no explanation for it. There is never anyone in that room when the light is seen, at least no living person.

Another ghost walks the hall of the house too, though not often. This is also a girl. No one seems to know who she is, or her history, but she has beautiful long hair, and she wanders from room to room, hairbrush in hand, crying, "Please comb my hair, please comb my hair."

Mrs. Fitch, who is not superstitious, has never seen the girl with the hairbrush, but she has heard another ghost, and he, or she, became so annoying she set to work and exorcised it in her own manner.

"He was a harmless ghost," Mrs. Fitch said. "He didn't appear and frighten anyone, but he waited until everyone was in bed and then began pulling trunks around the attic floor."

"There would be three steps," she continued, "then the sound of a trunk being dragged around, then three more steps, and again the dragging."

"It was intriguing at first, but then it became annoying. We couldn't sleep. So I went up in the attic and rearranged all the trunks. That must have confounded him because he hasn't made a sound since."

The trunk dragger may have had a literary, or perhaps, religious bent, also. One time Mrs. Fitch found in the attic a bed of leaves, an open bible, and a half burned candle in the leaves.

"I took them away quickly," she said. "Imagine a candle on leaves. The house might have been set on fire."

It is said that each year, on a moonlit night in May, a coach can be heard approaching the mansion, and if one listens closely the sound of violins can be heard emanating from the oval ballroom. Graybeards in the Town of Livingston say the coach belonged to Joseph Bonaparte in whose honor one of the gayest parties was given by the Widow Mary.

Not too many years ago on the eve of Decoration Day, the Fitches were entertaining guests at cards in the living room. The evening was getting late and a southerly breeze swept the broad expanse of the Hudson to the West, when Mr. Fitch and another gentleman who had gone upstairs, appeared in the room with guns. "Did you hear that noise?" they asked excitedly, and went hurriedly through the front door and drove about the estate in a car, using the lights to probe the long driveway.

Questioned on their return, Mr. Fitch said that both he and his guest distinctly heard the sound of a "metal-wheeled carriage coming up the driveway." Older residents of Livingston would nod their heads solemnly and agree it was Joseph Bonaparte returning for the Widow Mary's party in his honor.

Henry Livingston, Mary's husband, died while in Europe. His body was shipped back to the United States in a lead coffin and buried in a tomb not far from the mansion house. There were two other coffins, both wooden, in the tomb.

A story spread through the countryside that one of the wooden coffins contained the Livingston jewels and family heirlooms. In the summer of 1913, the tomb was broken into.

Henry's leaden coffin was punctured with a sharp object, a second coffin was smashed and its human contents strewn about the floor of the tomb. The third coffin vanished completely. Did it contain the jewels??? The story has never been answered.

For many years the old homestead had a caretaker whom we will call George, as many of his descendants still till the Livingston township soil.

He told awesome stories of opening the door of the place and viewing a bearded old man walking down the front stairs.

Among the many eerie happenings in the Widow Mary's Place is a particular door that will not close. First, felt-covered bricks were placed before it, but in the morning it was open. It was locked and bolted in the hours before midnight, but by the light of early dawn it stood completely ajar, moved by some ghostly hand, perhaps, but no one can definitely say.

If a south wind sweeps up the Hudson on May evenings, a visitor to the old homestead could meet a bearded old man dancing on the lawn to the music of violins, or hear the squeaking, crunching sounds of coach wheels on the gravel path as the Widow Mary entertains her friends.

Years ago the great manor house burned. The tile roof collapsed, but the sturdy walls and columns still remain . . . a ghostly monument of its glamorous mystic past.

CHAPTER 8

The Dog Collar

Do animals have souls as people do and somewhere, perhaps, a life after death? This may sound strange, even foolish, and I would never have given it much thought if I hadn't had two unusual, unexplained experiences.

I am one of those fortunate pet-owners who had a sixteen-year-long companionship with a wonderful dog - an English setter named "Dash"; a handsome, faithful pet and an excellent hunter.

Sixteen years is a good life span for a dog, and one of the grimmest days I ever remember was when I had to take my blind, helpless and suffering old companion to the "vet" to be put to sleep. He was buried in the small animal cemetery on the grounds of the vet's hospital. Perhaps I should have put him to rest on the hillside of our farm, where he had roamed in his prime.

His passing had left a great void in our lives. He had been so much a part of us, and without him the old farmhouse seemed lonesome and depressing for a long time. Then one day, when my wife and I had driven up from the city, parking the car outside of the garage, I was drawn to a spot of lilies-of-the-valley in the shade of an old lilac bush in front of the house. I thought my eyes were deceiving me when I saw Dash's collar partially hidden in the lush green ground cover. How had it gotten there? The dog, wearing his collar with its brass license tag, had been buried at the vet's animal cemetery. I picked up the dark brown leather object, carried it to the house, and hung it on a long, rusty nail in the workshop where I kept tools, paints and garden implements.

For a long time I sat in the rocking chair, on the front porch, as my thoughts wandered over the sixteen years - happy years - I had spent with my faithful companion. How had his leather collar gotten to the dense ground cover under the lilac bush? Finally I went into the house, picked up the telephone and called the vet, "Doc" Smith, a family friend, and explained the strange find to him. Doc, equally mystified, had no explanation as to how the collar had gotten from the burying ground at his place, five miles away, to rest under the lilac bush below the porch at our house.

Many years went by. Then I wrote a lengthy piece about my great old dog. It had been sent out to four or five magazines, always to be returned with a cold "No, thank you" rejection slip. My secretary thought the material was too far in the past to interest a publisher, and I was beginning to agree with her reasoning. It was sent out once more, perhaps my last effort to place it.

We had come up for the weekend again. The large one-acre lawn had to be mowed once more before fall and winter would take over. I took the mower back to the workshop to place it in a corner near the long, rusty nail on which the dog's collar had been hanging for many years. Just as I was turning around to go inside to rest up from my garden work, the dog collar jumped off the nail, landing right at my feet. Strange, I thought, as I picked it up to hang it in its place.

The next day, in the morning mail, I received a letter from the editor of *Outdoor Life* magazine, informing me that they had accepted my story, "Profile of an English Setter," including a substantial check. (The story was later chosen to be included in the anthology, "The Best Sports Stories 1974," published by E. P. Dutton Co.).

It seemed a strange coincidence that, after so many years, Dash's moldy, leather collar had leaped from its accustomed place on the nail in the workshop, falling at my feet the day before I was informed of the acceptance of his long-overdue eulogy. Since that day I still wonder - do animals have souls and a life after death? Was it perhaps Dash's spirit that revisited his happy hunting ground to give me a message? This odd telekinetic experience took me from the ranks of the skeptics.

Birds in hand after a day in the Berkshires,
Dash and I tired but content.

Two pheasants flushed just after I took this picture.

Dash

CHAPTER 9

The Golden Watch

Over the mantelpiece in our New York City apartment hangs a lovely oil painting of yellow ducklings swimming in a pond. A very fine piece of art done by a post-impressionist painter in Paris at the turn of the century. It is not only very beautiful, but also a conversation piece. This story leads back into the past when my family lived in Zittau, a thousand-year-old town, at the slopes of the Sudeten mountains. It is far from the tourist path in the southeast corner of Saxony, at one time a small kingdom bordering Czechoslovakia. Zittau has a great historical past, but no special fame except for a few savants and artists that have been born there and made a name for themselves in the world. My family lived there for generations and my grandfather was a wealthy merchant and highly esteemed burgher. He was already quite an old man when the first world war engulfed the nations.

At that time I was fourteen years old and about to be confirmed in the Lutheran church. My grandfather had three grandsons. The older two had each received a beautiful gold watch from him as a confirmation present, but as my turn came there were no gold watches to be had. All the gold coins and jewelry had been gathered by the government to be melted into ingots to help pay the enormous costs of this dreadful war; so, at my confirmation Grandfather patted me on the shoulder:

"Well, my boy," he said with a sad look in his eyes, "I wanted to give you a fine watch as I have given your cousins. Unfortunately, this I cannot do for there are none to be bought. But I promise you I will make good for this later when the war is over. I will see to it that you get your share, equal to my other grandsons."

I was not upset too much at that time. The war finally ended, plunging the nation into the most gigantic inflation and wiping out all my grandfather's wealth. Years later he died - a lovable, impoverished old man.

Time went by and some years ago my son Bob, then about 14 years old, had a summer job working for our friends and neighbors, Paul and Phyllis Tilson. There he mowed their extensive lawn, weeded the garden, painted the green shutters of their lovely old farmhouse in Old Chatham, a small upstate New York Village nestled in the foothills of the Berkshires.

One day he was asked to help clean out the barn. Among other things bound for the junkyard was a collection of old paintings, unfinished or badly damaged canvases that had been left to Mrs. Tilson by her father, a well-known American landscape painter. He had died a few years before in his late 90's. The old paintings, some done by other artists (friends) and probably traded for his own work, were now relegated to the barn. No longer of any value to the Tilson's, the dusty old canvases were simply rotting away. As they rummaged together marking the old canvases to be discarded, they came upon an unusually beautiful painting in a wide goldleaf frame, depicting yellow ducks swimming in a pond. But since it

Oil by Rudolph Schramm

was not the work of her father, Mrs. Tilson was about to throw it on the rubbish heap when she and Bob gave it a last glance. They read the signature of the artist and the brass marker attached to the frame. It read: Prof. Rudolph Schramm. Zittau, year 1900.

"Zittau is my father's home town," Bob pointed out to Phyllis, who had also heard me mention the place once or twice.

"We must show it to your parents," Mrs. Tilson announced, "They might like it. So let's not throw it away but take it to the house."

The following Friday my wife and I arrived at the Tilson house to pick up our son so he could spend the weekend with us at our nearby farmhouse. When we were shown the strange discovery I was absolutely flabbergasted. Not only did we love the painting, but I recalled that many years ago my father had mentioned the name Rudolph Schramm to me when I was a youngster and we went sketching together in the countryside. On such an occasion my father had suggested to me that I become a famous painter like Rudolph Schramm whom he greatly admired. But I had not heard that name mentioned again for about 50 years.

"Take it - it's yours," said Phyllis Tilson to us as we were leaving. I promptly reported the strange discovery in a letter to my mother, then still living in my old home-town. Her reply was equally prompt and she wrote:

"My dear boy, you are very, very lucky indeed to come into possession of a painting by Rudolph Schramm. He is the greatest artist our town ever produced. Not only was he famous, but he was also your grandfather's godchild. The old man was very close to the Schramm family. And to top it all, your favorite Aunt Martha came close to marrying Rudolph's brother."

I checked the name and the fame of the artist in New York galleries, museums, and in art books, eagerly pursuing information about the mysterious gift, and here are some of the results:

"Professor Rudolph Schramm, 1874-1929, Born in Zittau. His paintings hang in many national art muse-ums in Dresden, Karlsruhe, Munich, Paris and Boston. He won the gold medal for fine art in Paris in 1900.

What had brought this great painting into our hands? It had come from an obscure town no one had ever heard of and it had travelled thousands of miles, perhaps first to Paris where the artist probably had traded it with Phyllis Tilson's father, then a young American painter in France. He must have taken it with him on his return to New York City where he spent most of his life. Then it came to rest in the Tilson barn, lost and forgotten there in the foothills of the Berkshires, thousands of miles from the town on the slopes of the Sudeten mountains.

And here it fell into my hands. An unbelievably strange coincidence or a mystic miracle?

I cannot convince myself that this fine painting, many times more valuable to us than a gold watch, got to us by mere coincidence. The circumstances are too fantastic to imagine. I believe the guiding spirit of my lovable old grandfather, determined to make good his promise of the gold watch which he had been unable to give me, conducted this almost unbelievable transaction by ways and means far beyond my comprehension.

CHAPTER 10

Spooks at the Manor House

It is a rare occurrence to rub elbows with royalty. Although I never rubbed elbows, I did enjoy a long personal correspondence with his late Royal Highness, Prince Ernst Heinrich von Sachsen. He was at that time the last surviving son of King Friedrich August of Saxony, who had abdicated his throne at the end of World War I. The Prince had written the story of his life, *Mein Lebensweg* (My Life's Journey) "From Royal Palace to Farm Cottage," published by Paul List Verlag, Munich, and I had translated part of this charming book in an effort to promote its publication in the United States.

The author told a fascinating story, starting as a young prince in the romantic castles and palaces of his family, which had ruled over the ancient kingdom of Saxony for over 500 years. The Prince was a sportsman and had been a cavalry officer during the First World War. Later, in peacetime, his life was threatened. Royalty was hated by the Nazis, who once condemned him to death before a firing squad but did not dare to carry out the execution of a German prince. At the end of World War II, he was even more hated by the Communists, who finally forced him to leave his ancestral home.

Deprived of his vast holdings, he became a farmer in Ireland, exiled forever from his homeland. The Prince had studied agriculture at the University of Breslau, where part of his curriculum had included a year of practical farm experience. He chose a large farming estate, Nährschutz, in Silesia. It is here that the worldly, educated Prince, who had never mentioned any ghostly experiences at the many ancient castles his family owned, had an eerie encounter with the supernatural. What follows is my translation of a chapter in his book.

Nährschutz was a small village near the river Oder. The massive manor house and courtyard were located close to the road. It had been built in the 18th century. There was some association with my family as it had been the stopover for my illustrious ancestor, August der Starke (the strong) on his way to Warsaw. (In 1734 he became King of Poland, a country hundreds of miles from his Saxon domain.) I received a warm welcome from the family; Mr. Strach, his much younger, musically inclined wife, two grown sons, and a 17-year-old daughter, Ilse.

My quarters were on the rear wing of the house. I noticed that no one else lived in this section though it seemed very attractive, as it faced the garden. I soon felt at home here, where I was to be introduced to the secrets of agriculture. My oldest sister, Margarethe, had wished her black poodle on me, because she was going on a lengthy voyage. He slept in my room at night. One night, near dawn, I was awakened by an unusual whimpering sound coming from the poodle. I turned on the light and saw a strange, large black dog at my bedside. At the same time I heard sounds from the perturbed poodle hiding under the desk, frightened by the presence of its weird rival. I jumped out of bed and reached for the black dog, which then dissolved into nebulous nothing. My poodle, shaking in terror, could not be coaxed into leaving his hiding place. Since I had never had such an eerie experience, I persuaded myself that all this had been my imagination. But soon I was to learn otherwise.

Later, as I was talking with the daughter of the house, she confessed that there were spooks in the back wing of the mansion. I had to promise not to mention this to her parents. She also told me that recently a black dog had suddenly appeared at her side as she and her brother were descending the stairs. When she tried to reach for him, he disappeared into nothing. Since we all had this mutual experience, I ceased to be a skeptic, and we decided to check the archives at the nearby town of Koben, searching for earlier records of spooks at Nährschutz. We were happy to locate some 18th century information about a black dog and a ghostly woman haunting the manor at that time.

Soon I was to get more hushed-up information from the younger members of the Strach family. Many years before, a former owner of the estate had fallen down the steps leading to the main hall while in a drunken stupor, thereby breaking his neck. Ever since his death, an invisible person has walked nightly from an adjoining room into the hall. I considered this most ridiculous. I had no wish to become further acquainted with manor house spooks. I had had my share with the black dog and also with an illuminated nebulous globe that once floated about in my room.

During the following weeks all returned to normal. I spent much of the time in the evening reading and writing, and I often enjoyed the spirited company of the younger set. An attractive young girl of Ilse's age had come to visit, and we all had a jolly good time together.

One evening, after the parents had retired, we were gathered in the spacious hall, sipping good wine, exchanging yarns, joking and laughing. Time had gone by fast, and we were hardly aware that midnight was approaching. Then we heard the tense voice of Fred Strach:

"He will be coming soon."

"Who will be coming soon?" I asked, not expecting another guest at that hour.

"Well, the man who fell to his death here a long time ago. He roams about here every night."

"Let him come, then," I replied. We were all in high spirits, and I was not over eager to respond to such nonsense.

"You will soon experience it," Ilse said. "He will come."

I purposely diverted the conversation to another topic, but soon Fred interrupted me.

"Now he's coming - there, from the next room."

We were all silent. First I heard him very softly, then louder and louder. As the distinct footsteps of a man approached us, I sat frozen, staring into the direction of the invisible phenomenon. It seemed hard to believe, but the unseen person existed. The steps became firmer and louder. One had the feeling that the walking ghost would soon be in our midst. Then he stopped. Nobody dared to move or utter a sound. It was ghastly. All this lasted perhaps fifteen seconds, then we heard more footsteps right in front of us. At last he retreated, following the same path he had come, returning to the adjoining room. Gradually, the sounds became less and less pronounced until they stopped.

"Yes," said Fred, "That was him. He comes night after night, year after year, for as long as we can remember. He comes in and he goes out."

I was quite upset by this experience and could hardly fall asleep that night. Fully aware that something unusual had taken place, I became more and more convinced of the existence of psychic phenomena. I had heard of ghostly women who were supposed to haunt old castles, I had heard of poltergeists, but I had never, ever experienced anything like this encounter. Why was this man, or perhaps only his footsteps, banished to this house, and for how long a time? What was it that he had to atone for? All this remains a mystery.

CHAPTER 11

Castle Bronner

This piece has been graciously released to me by H.R.H. Princess Virginia von Sachsen, widow of the late H.R.H. Prince Ernst Henrich von Sachsen, who died while stag hunting several years ago. The first part is set between the two world wars while the prince was living at his castle, Moritzburg. It concludes sometime later after the second world war, with the prince an exile from his homeland. Unlike the previous chapters, this eerie but authentic story about a 14th century castle has not been previously published.

"Yesterday I had an unusual, fascinating conversation with a retired priest, who lived for a time at Castle Bronner, near Beuron in Southern Germany. At that castle, he experienced an incredible case of haunting. You must hear it in his own words." With this introduction, the chaplain of the Prince's castle at Moritzburg arranged for the retired priest to visit the Prince.

A short, elderly man, wearing a dark suede jacket, entered the Prince's study on the following Sunday afternoon. After an exchange of a few words while greeting him and making him comfortable, he quickly came to the point, and for three hours immersed the Prince and his sons in the eerie events at Castle Bronner. The beautiful, life-like portrait of the Prince's ancestor, Elector August III (son of the illustrious August the Strong), looked down upon them. The magnificent red, blue and gold tapestry glowed in the brilliant May sunlight. All this, however, made very little impression on the small priest, who looked at them with piercing eyes, as he concentrated on his narration of the ghostly experience at Castle Bronner, located hundreds of miles to the southwest in the upper Danube Valley.

"I rented living quarters right at the Castle Bronner because I had fallen in love with its enchanting location, solitude and romantic atmosphere. Nothing unusual happened during my first few weeks at the place. One afternoon, while reading and taking in the magnificent view from my window, I heard a very strange rumble and clicking and clatter. It seemed as if something had fallen from the wall and then continued rolling on the floor. The racket steadily gained momentum, now sounding more like large stones rolling. This lasted for about two minutes, then it suddenly stopped. I rushed from my room to the hall, as the sound had seemed to have centered very close by. I found nothing out of order. Inspecting outside in the castle court and on the floor above me, I found nothing seemed changed in any way. Needless to say, I was very disturbed. I remember having read time and again about similar phenomena, especially the goings-on at the parish of the priest of Ars in France.

It seemed only natural for me, as a priest, to pray and I selected the Great Exorcism. Then I went for a lengthy walk through the woods, where I also prayed from the

Breviary. After supper I went over to the lectern and as the evening went on, almost forgot all about the unpleasant happenings.

But then it started again, with greatly increased force. The rolling and booming and high pitched clanking were combined with shrill, eerie, unearthly wails. Almost paralyzed, I put on my stole and reached for the holy water. Then it happened. The door of my study was torn wide open with a terrifying crash and a gigantic ball of stone rolled into my room, accompanied by two large copper kettles bouncing and clanking against one another. I fled into the farthest corner of my room, made the sign of the cross and sprinkled holy water. Finally, the three terrifying things that I had never seen before retreated toward the hall door accompanied by eerie shrieks and cries.

Now, for the first time in my life, I had heard and seen with my own eyes a powerful spook or poltergeist and I became numb, almost paralyzed. I must admit that I did not have the courage to go outside of my room into the hall. I spent the night, mostly praying, trying to clear my mind and collect my thoughts, anticipating a new outbreak at any moment. But nothing happened, and Castle Bronner, surrounded by its beautiful lush forest, was resting peacefully.

I wondered if this spook had been directed to me personally. And I tried to analyze what had caused it and what may have been its purpose. I did not rule out satanic influences, but was more inclined to believe that some lost souls could have something to do with it. Therefore I read the Mass of the Dead at Castle Bronner the next morning. After this there was perfect peace for two full weeks and I attributed this to my reading the Mass. But then one evening it began again. To my horror I heard the shrill shrieks and wails which I had heard before, combined with the rolling, roar and rumble as if heavy vehicles were moving up and down the hall. This time I was somewhat calmer than during the previous manifestations. I read again the Exorcism, and special prayers for the dead. Suddenly a stone came through the open window though without causing damage. I closed the window. Suddenly chairs turned over and when I straightened them up, they fell over again. My Breviary slid from the table and when I picked it up it was covered with what seemed to be a slimy spattered saliva. Then more stones came through the closed window without causing the slightest damage. The entire disturbance lasted about 10 minutes, then there was silence.

Again I remember having read that similar phenomena sometimes occurred not only in ancient castles, but also in recently built development houses.

Why had the exorcism failed? I was especially upset that my Breviary, the every day prayer book of a priest had been soiled with filthy spittle and saliva. These circumstances convinced me that satanic forces had been involved. I carefully cleaned up the holy book, blessed it and sprinkled it with holy water. Never, ever has it been touched or defiled again.

Now since blissful peace and quiet had settled over my quarters, I contemplated if it would not be better and wiser to leave Bronner. This of course would have been capitulation, and as a clergyman I felt that this would be wrong. Perhaps it was designed for me, the priest, to leave the haunted castle. So I decided at least for the time being to stay on.

The evening after my contemplation, I was sitting in my study reading. I suddenly thought that I heard a delicate whisper. At first I attributed it to my imagination, a reaction perhaps to my strained nerves. The whispering continued and gradually clearly understandable words were formed:

"It is I who am banished here at Bronner." At first I

began to question the state of my own mind. It seemed impossible, utterly unbelievable to me. In order to regain my own equilibrium, I began to pray. Then again I heard the whispering. Now the words were clearly understandable:

"It is I, the knight who has been banished here." (The priest had mentioned the name, but the Prince had forgotten it over the years.)

I strained all my courage and wit and replied, "Why?"

"Because I have committed a murder here that cannot be atoned."

"When have you lived and where?"

"Here in Bronner in the 14th century."

"Where did you commit the murder?"

"Here in Bronner."

"Whom did you murder?" There was no answer. "Have you buried your victim?"

"Yes."

"Where?"

"Near the well of the castle."

"Can you be helped?" No answer. This ended the conversation. I asked myself if perhaps all this had been my imagination. But the voice had been so clear and convincing that it left no trace of doubt in my mind. I had been perfectly calm. It seemed as if I had been sitting in a confessional box listening to the confession of a murderer.

A few days later I experienced again the now familiar whisper which started out like a faint hissing. This time I took the initiative and asked, "Who are you?"

"I am the wife of the murder victim."

"Have you also been banished here?"

"Yes."

"Was the knight your lover?"

"Yes."

"You have killed your husband because he was in your way?"

Castle Bronner

Castle Moritzburg

"Yes."

"Can the murder be atoned?" No answer. "Where have you buried him?"

"Beside the well."

"Give me a clear description of the exact spot." The designation followed.

"Have you something to do with the tumultuous haunting?" No answer.

"Do you know that I am a priest?"

"Yes."

"Is there someone interested in driving me away from here?"

"Yes."

"Who?" No answer. "Are you expecting help from me?" No answer.

With this information it was clear to me that it would be of the greatest importance to locate the skeleton of the murder victim. This would give me absolute proof that I had actually conversed with the murderers. Then perhaps more information could be obtained about the haunting of the castle.

I decided to start the excavation. It was a beautiful day in July. If I had only known what I was getting into I would not have gone ahead with the project.

I started to dig at the designated spot. The ground was extremely hard and stony and it was strenuous work for me. But I had several good reasons why I undertook this laborious project all by myself. After three days I had dug down about three feet and I was hopeful for success, especially since the ground had become less rigid and began to give.

At that moment I suddenly heard from all around me loud hissing and whistling sounds. I was spat upon in my face so severely that I could not look out of my eyes. Then I was pummeled with fierce punches from all directions. Stones fell upon me and my diggings from all sides. I fell down to earth, face to the ground and called out loud the words of Christ: "Vade Satanas (Begone Satan.)"

Completely exhausted and almost close to unconsciousness I remained lying on the ground until the vicious attack ceased. Then I filled in the digging and left Bronner forever."

Later, the Prince himself was to have a supernatural experience at Castle Bronner. In the following passage, he recounts it in his own words:

Years later, after World War II, when I (had) found asylum in Sigmaringen in the French occupied section, I had an occasion to visit there. At other times - while stag hunting near Beuron at the opposite banks of the Danube, I again saw the imposing citadel in the distance rising from its surrounding dark green spruce forest.

Bronner is more than a castle. It is a fortified medieval burg, high above the Danube valley, isolated from its surroundings and only connected to the world by a narrow dirt road leading through the dense forest.

Now uninhabited, it had during the Hitler days occasionally been used as a residence by high ranking Nazi officials. At the end of the war, when it became part of the French occupied zone of Germany, a detachment of their Moroccan troops was quartered there at the castle. This project, however, was soon abandoned. The detachment left the place, terrorized in hasty flight, as they had experienced uncanny, eerie hauntings. As the French officers told me, the Moroccans reported that an invisible phantom had been walking around, leaving deep footprints in the rocks. Some even reported that these footprints had glowed on with fire for some time afterwards. The French command took notice of these matters and promptly discontinued using the castle for quartering troops.

The officers of the French command, located at Sigmaringen, became very much interested in inspecting Castle Bronner, wishing to find out if it was really haunted.

(The anti-Nazi, anti-Communist Prince had been in good rapport with the French government, which had given him asylum from his homeland now ruled by the Communists. He had become well acquainted with the French officers whose language he spoke fluently.)

We made arrangements to drive to Castle Bronner. Unfortunately, we failed to get access to the premises because the keys, supposedly in care at the nearby village, could not be located. Therefore, we were only able to view the place from the outside and let our imaginations wander. My own mind wandered back to the afternoon in Moritzburg where the emeritus priest had held us in suspense telling us his experiences here at the Castle Bronner that seemed almost unbelievable to me at that time.

Dusk was beginning to settle over the sturdy medieval stronghold and the forest began to sink into darkness. This reminded us of our return trip and we walked towards our cars, parked in the woods.

"Qu'est-ce que C'est que ca?" (What is this?) I heard a voice and soon after:

"C'est une Pierre, qui est tombée du ciel." (This is a stone that has fallen from the sky.)

"Encore une." (And one more.)

And now several stones clattered through the spruce tops, crashing to earth uncomfortably close to us.

This started a lively, excited discussion among the French officers. Very much impressed by this, we all agreed: "C'était produit par un phantome du chateau de Bronner." (Caused by the phantom of Castle Bronner.)

Since than I have had reports from Sigmaringen that now and then people have come to Bronnen to get to the bottom of the various unexplained supernatural happenings there. Most of them have had frightening experiences and have chosen to leave Bronner as soon as they could.

CHAPTER 12

✑

The Guardian Angels

Are there any Guardian Angels? Perhaps there are,
(always have been and always will be). As long as man
has existed on this planet, he has believed that some
spiritual force influences his life, guiding him, protecting
him, punishing and destroying him. In ancient mythology gods and demi-gods personified such unknown
spirits. Primitive man as well as more sophisticated
religions all through the ages proclaim the presence of
spirits in some form or other. Orientals worship their
ancestors, pray to them at their altars to guide and help
their living descendants.

The Judeo-Christian religion believes in one God only,
but accepts the existence of angels: "Behold, I send an
angel before thee to keep thee in thy way," (Exodus
23:20); and the Roman Catholic Church recognizes
countless saints who specialize as guiding, inspiring,
protective spirits to mankind. Houses of worship display
images of angels.

While few people have ever claimed to have seen an
angel, their presence has been felt and professed by

innumerable creative people, renowned artists, composers, writers, scientists, inventors, leaders and discoverers. Some have openly and publicly admitted that their accomplishments were only made possible by some spiritual touch. Ordinary people like me, pursuing their regular daily lives, also admit the guidance and protection of spiritual intervention.

There are many others who scoff at such thoughts and arrogantly claim that they are the sole masters of their destinies, and their superior brain cells are fully responsible for their doings and misdoings. The word "inspiration" is related to the word "spirit." True, the gentle touch of a guardian angel is very subtle and often remains completely hidden. (However, simply because it cannot be seen, physically felt or heard, that does not prove that it does not exist. We do not hear or see the Boston Symphony or the World Series hundreds of miles away, though their sound waves are all around us. We must turn on a sensitive receiving instrument - a radio or a television set - to bring it to us and make it audible and visible to us.) Yet, there are moments in our lives when the touch of a guardian angel appears very evident and convincing. The two stories in this chapter recount experiences in our family that give dramatic evidence of intervention by unseen hands.

We had arrived by train at the Hudson railroad station and my wife and I drove along State Route 66 heading for our country house in Old Chatham for the weekend. It was late in the afternoon on a clear and sunny day as we approached the intersection where Route 66 crosses 9H, a busy section of U.S. Highway 9. We stopped the car as the traffic light had turned red. Shortly it changed to green and I stepped on the accelerator. At that moment my wife touched my arm.

"Don't go - don't go."

We would have dashed through the clear crossing in

our 8-cylinder car - but I jammed on the brakes. At that moment a heavy farm truck, loaded with crates of agricultural products recklessly roared through the red light. We had not seen it coming, as an embankment on the left obstructed the distant view of 9H. If I had proceeded, we both would have been killed in a total smash-up of our car. We were miraculously saved.

What induced my wife to ask me not to go ahead? What made me heed her seemingly unreasonable request not to proceed through the green "Go" signal? Here we both felt the clear and convincing action of a benevolent spirit - a guardian angel.

The truck thundered away in the distance as we finally drove on our way, shaken by the grim encounter that could have been our last moment alive.

This clearly marked and properly signalled intersection had been the scene of a fatal accident a few years before. Our good neighbor Mike B. and his teenage son had been killed instantly, and Mrs. B. had been severely injured. In this case, however, the young driver had heedlessly driven through the red light and a monstrous tank truck had crushed their car into a mass of metallic pulp. Ironically, it was a milk-tank truck that had ended the life of our neighbors, a small dairy farmer and his son. Was it perhaps their spirits from another world that had intervened and saved us from certain death, as it had ended their days on this earth?

Another encounter, less dramatic yet just as mysterious, is the story of my grandfather's desk; today the most precious of the family antiques in our New York City apartment.

When I was a young boy, it belonged to my favorite maiden aunt who lived in a modest fourth-storey apartment in a quiet tree-shaded residential section of Dresden, then the picturesque and romantic capital of the kingdom of Saxony. Even as a small child I had a

The secretary.

great attachment to this piece of furniture with its many drawers and shelves. It should really be called a secretary. It became a desk only when the writing panel was unlocked and folded out, revealing an assortment of small drawers and shelves. It had belonged to my grandfather, Secretary of Finance in the small Kingdom. He had died many years before I was born. My lovable, generous maiden aunt had told me many times, "This secretary will someday belong to you, the son of the oldest son of your distinguished grandfather. I will see to it that it goes to you - and you will leave it to your son."

Years later I went to live in the United States and I had forgotten all about my grandfather's secretary. The last time I saw my aunt was during one of my short trips abroad; a few years before the nations were engulfed in the dreadful second world war. Towards the end of the war, my aging aunt was taken to an old-age home - set up in an antiquated chateau not too far from Dresden. She was allowed to bring some of her possessions with her, including grandfather's secretary.

Only a few weeks after she had given up her lifelong residence in the capital of Saxony, Dresden was unexpectedly destroyed by thousands of bombs dropped on this unfortunate, defenseless city. In this holocaust, 300,000 of its civilian population were killed, burned to death by phosphorous bombs or buried alive in the demolished buildings, churches, museums, and hospitals for war prisoners.

Years later, after a feeble reconstruction effort had been made, I passed the site of my aunt's former residence. It was a heap of rubble. Miraculously, my aunt had survived several miles away from Dresden in a small room surrounded by her few worldly possessions, among them my grandfather's secretary.

Some years later she died; her death perhaps hastened by post-war misery and chaos, (undernourishment, inadequate care and lack of heat in the lonesome home of the aged). With travel conditions almost paralyzed, my sister went to bury her in the family plot. Disposing of the small legacy, she made arrangements for Grandfather's secretary to be shipped to her home which she shared with our aging mother. The secretary had already been removed and relegated to the cellar by the management of the institution. Shipping facilities were almost non-existent. But she did not despair, and managed to get the venerable piece of furniture to her home, using the most primitive forms of transportation - horse-drawn wagons, a riverboat and finally an open railroad freight car. With the economy of the war-torn country in complete collapse, her payment for this incredible shipment had been made possible with the aid of some packages of American cigarettes; a highly valued currency at that time that I had managed to get to her in a small food package. Grandfather's desk had now joined other family antiques in the apartment where my mother and sister lived behind the Iron Curtain in East Germany.

Years later, in 1964, my mother died at the age of 93. Then at last I succeeded with great difficulty in obtaining permission to enter the "Zone." I had not been able to see my family for over 20 years, and I was finally permitted to come and bury my mother's ashes.

Entering through "Checkpoint Charlie" I got into East Berlin, still, in parts, a wasteland of ruins and rubble. My home town, far at the southern border of East Germany, was in surprisingly good shape. There my sister lived in her comfortable but small apartment.

I was fully aware that I was now in a communist police state. As a visitor from the outside world I was treated politely, but I carefully watched my words at all times. My sister wanted me to have part of my mother's legacy. However, it was strictly "verboten" to take any antiques out of the country. A cup of Meissen porcelain, if found in my luggage, would have placed me behind bars.

After my return to the United States I received a message from my sister - a complete surprise. A court had decided that I, the legal beneficiary of half of my mother's estate, would be entitled to receive my share - some of my mother's collection of Meissen china, my grandmother's beautiful antique sewing table and my grandfather's secretary. My sister was now permitted to ship these items to me after a thorough inspection. The furniture had to be properly crated; a frustrating task as it was almost impossible to obtain wood for the crates. Finally it was shipped to a Baltic seaport and from there by boat to the United States. Months later I received a notification that the freighter, *Finlandia,* was to dock in Brooklyn, bringing my inheritance to our shores. We were overjoyed. Once more, however, disaster was approaching.

My teenage son, home from school with a bad cold, heard the alarming news over the radio that the good ship *Finlandia* was afire at the pier, a total loss of ship and cargo. We were deeply shaken by this disheartening event. After the miraculous survival, the tremendous efforts to protect and transport it, Grandfather's desk was now turned to ashes in the bowels of the burning ship. Two days later, we received a notice from the shipping broker that my belongings were on their way to us by truck. Only a few crates had been set ashore moments before the fire had broken out. Our shipment was among those few items.

It is hard to conceive that the fate of Grandfather's desk was a mere accumulation of coincidences. I believe it was a miracle, guided by the action of some guardian angel. Perhaps the determined spirit of my lovable maiden aunt had something to do with this fantastic odyssey.

I could recount more such startling events, and I am

sure I am not alone in recognizing the unexplained inter-
ferences by mysterious forces. More often, though, the
touch of such spirits may remain unrecognized by us. I
could not have written this piece, or any other published
material and attributed them arrogantly to products of
my brain cells alone. Some outside powers have guided
me and I prefer to call them guardian angels.

CHAPTER 13

The Rope Bed

There had been no ghostly activity in our house for a number of years, so we presumed that perhaps the spirits had become disinterested and bored with us. This, however, proved to be the wrong conclusion.

Another midsummer weekend had come to an end. Our children, Bob and his wife Ginny, had been our house guests. They were about to start on their return trip. They faced a long drive to Maryland, stopping in New York City to drop my wife, Ruth, at our town apartment. She had to be at her office Monday morning, while I was spending another day in the country to finish up some chores that had not been completed.

Because of the long trip ahead of them, they had scheduled their departure for the early afternoon. Packing and loading their small station wagon always involved some hustle and bustle. Their elusive white cat, hiding in the bushes, had to be captured, and there had been a hasty last minute trip to the vegetable garden to pick a few zucchini that had grown in great abundance during the hot, humid summer.

I waved them goodbye as they drove off. It had been a happy but exhausting weekend. As I returned to the lonesome and quiet house I felt tired, and a short rest on the couch in our cool, informal dining-sitting room seemed inviting and appropriate to me. I always considered this room adjoining the kitchen my favorite. Located in the oldest section of the house, it has all the markings of its 200-year-old origin. An antique wood stove, looking like a miniature Chinese temple, provides adequate heat during the cold season when we drive up to spend a winter weekend. The brick chimney painted white, was decorated with some 18th century powder horns. A shotgun spreads out over the door leading to the kitchen. It came to good use when a woodchuck discovered our flower beds or our small vegetable garden, and we had to protect the tender products of our hard labor.

Stretched out on the comfortable couch, I glanced at the ceiling where six handhewn mahogany-colored beams supported wide rough pine boards, still showing the straight ripping of the up and down saw. The 200-year-old timber had been cut before the circular saw was invented. Above this was our best guest room which had been occupied by our children during their stay.

I was just about to doze off when I became aware of some strange sounds right above the ancient ceiling. I was too tired to be disturbed, too drowsy even to analyze the cause of the reverberation. I must have been asleep for some time when the sounds above me awakened me again. This time they were quite pronounced. It seemed as if someone was walking around the old rope bed (now equipped with spring and mattress for greater comfort). I listened carefully. Someone, perhaps a woman, was walking around the bed in short, light steps just as if to make the bed in the deserted guest room. The unusual noise stopped again. We had been used to strange

Rope bed in our guest room.

Our dining room with cast iron parlor stove.

goings-on in our old house and had accepted the occasional presence of a ghost. Just as I was about to doze again, the sound of light footsteps, centered exactly above me, was heard pacing around the old rope bed. Who could have come into the house? It seemed a logical thought as we rarely lock the front door. It seems unnecessary in country houses. Still, someone could easily have come in and gotten up to the second floor, roaming about undisturbed by its sleepy owner. Could it be a burglar? The idea seemed remote, but I felt I should investigate.

I got up from the comforting couch and reached for the double-barrelled shotgun. There were a few shells in the drop-leaf desk next to the kitchen door. I broke the gun and inserted two #4 shells into the barrels. Now, with gun under my arm, I headed for the hallway staircase. I felt rather foolish. Never before had I policed our peaceful home armed with a deadly weapon!

I pushed the guest room door open. Nobody was there as I faced the empty room looking at the unmade rope bed. Our guests had left in quite a hurry and Ginny, who always made up the bed before departure, had not done so this Sunday afternoon. I went through all the upstairs rooms and found no intruder. Could it have been a poltergeist? It seemed to me the only feasible explanation for the mysterious footsteps. But why would a poltergeist sound like a woman making an unmade bed? Had it perhaps been the spirit of our house ghost, Mary Chase, the prim and disciplined Quaker maiden who had occasionally given evidence of her presence in various ways? Perhaps she felt that Ginny should have been better organized in attending to her duties and should have made the guest room bed before leaving. I could not come up with a better explanation. So I let it go at that as I settled down in a comfortable rocking chair on the porch. After all, it had been a lovely day, and a glorious

sunset beyond the Catskill mountain range in the far
distance was in the offing.

CHAPTER 14

∽

The Bright Light

Far away from our nearest neighbors, our isolated old farmhouse overlooks the Hudson Valley from a thousand-foot elevation, with the Catskill Mountains 60 miles away on the western horizon. Because of its appealing view, we spend much of our leisure time lounging in the sunny spots or in the shade of the tall elms on our lawn. Perhaps the most enchanting hours there are in the late summer evenings under a starry sky.

On one of those cool, silent evenings, August 21, 1976, my wife, Ruth, and I, along with our weekend guest, Joy Edwards, an attractive English art dealer, were enjoying the soothing silence. Only the distant barking of a dog or the pleasing sound of cowbells from a nearby pasture occasionally interrupted the silence of the hillside. However, this peaceful evening was to provide us with a strange, unexplainable phenomenon.

It was shortly before midnight. Joy and I, reclining in our lawnchairs, were facing west; the white clapboard house was on our right. My wife had just gotten up from her chair to study the clear sky, hoping to see a shooting star. Then suddenly from the east came a ball of light. It moved at high speed toward the west, then suddenly stopped. The entire lawn and the white house were instantly engulfed in what was almost bright daylight. The house itself was illuminated as if a powerful set of lights had been turned on like those used in the filming of Hollywood movies. It is hard to say how long it lasted, possibly only for a few moments. I jumped from my chair and ran toward the house, fearing that something inside had caused it. Actually, that did not make much sense, as the light obviously did not come from inside, but rather from the powerful illumination caused by the fireball. It lingered above our house. Then the light went off and, abruptly, the object veered off at a right angle, disappearing over the rooftop as it headed straight north.

The three of us were shocked and frightened. Never before had we witnessed such a strange sight. Was it perhaps a meteor, crashing down to earth somewhere in the distance? A meteor would move in a straight line earthward, without changing its path. My wife had gotten the best view of the mysterious, white illuminated body. Facing the eastern sky, she had had a perfect view of the fast-approaching object. Joy and I had only seen the fantastic effect it had on the house and the lawn, lighting them up as if it were daytime. Of course, lightning was out of the question on this clear, silent night. What could it have been?

Only once before had I heard of a somewhat similar though unrelated natural phenomenon my mother and sister had experienced many years before in Germany. They lived in a town below the Sudeten Mountains and had gone for an afternoon outing to a tavern on the top of a sandstone mountain called "The Oybin." The small inn was located next to the ruins of a Celestine monastery dating back to the 12th century. The high stone walls of the ancient gothic church had made this spot a favorite historic site.

Suddenly, out of the sky, a fireball, perhaps 10 to 12 feet in diameter, crashed down upon the ancient walls of the ruin, accompanied by tremendous, terrifying sounds of explosions. It bounced on the stone structure, leaped up and down from the ground to the wall like a huge volleyball, bounced inside the ruins and reappeared to race into the distant mountainsides. Needless to say, the two women were thoroughly frightened and rushed for shelter inside the tavern. There they discovered all the electric wiring had been destroyed. There was no light or telephone, but otherwise no damage had been done to the establishment. Heavy rain and wind soon followed, as a violent thunderstorm broke out.

My mother and sister often repeated the story of their startling experience. However, while this was a most unusual natural phenomenon, it is readily explainable as an electrical charge that had preceded the storm.

Our experience was of an entirely different nature. There was no thunderstorm anywhere. There was no sound only the fiery object coming from the eastern sky, halting above our place, turning at a right angle and disappearing toward the northern firmament. The next day we inquired in the village and among our neighbors, but nobody had seen anything. After our return to New York City, my wife called the Planetarium to report and to seek an explanation about our encounter. She received only a recorded message.

This occurrence remains a mystery to us. It seems logical to rule out the effect of an electric charge emanating from a clear, cloudless sky. We ruled out a meteor, because a meteor cannot change its course; it follows in a straight line. This leaves only one feasible explanation: Was it a UFO?

Where we saw the bright light.

Entrance to the Gothic ruin where the fireball bounced about.

CHAPTER 15

The Black Thing

Very much like people, some ghosts are benevolent, friendly and helpful, while others may be hostile, ugly, threatening. In the following pages we meet one of the latter kind, a demon that has frightened and tormented two sound and stable families and forced them to leave their home.

Today this haunted house is the home of an elderly, retired couple who have never been told about the eerie things that were experienced by the previous tenants. As far as I know, they have not encountered any paranormal activities since they took possession of their house.

Would it be fair to tell this story in a book, frightening the old couple and perhaps destroying the peace and contentment they are now enjoying? I agreed with the two families who provided me with this material that I would tell the story, but completely disguise names, dates and places. However, the actual haunting is reported word for word as it happened. Documented evidence from the two couples has been submitted to my editor, who has promised to keep it an absolute secret. By this procedure, full protection has been provided for the present owner of the house and no harm can be caused by publishing this story.

I have been in this house many years ago. There had been an advertisement in the *Chatham Courier*, the local newspaper, offering a Shaker wardrobe for sale. My wife, much interested in antiques, and also in dire need of additional closet space for our bedroom, decided to go and see the advertised piece. We made a telephone appointment and set out in our station wagon for Neversville, a half an hour's drive from our house. It was a beautiful August day and we had no problem finding the place. It was an old house, perhaps one of the oldest in the village, only a stone's throw away from a church of Greek revival architecture. The storey-and-a-half house, shaded by old Sugar Maples, looked cool and inviting. We walked along a flagstone path past a well-kept lawn and flower garden and knocked at the door. Mr. Cotter, a short bald-headed man with small blue eyes set close together in a pink, puffy face, opened the door.

"We came about the Shaker wardrobe," we explained as we were invited to enter a small, comfortable-looking living room, furnished mostly with Edwardian period pieces, including several overstuffed chairs protected by lace doilies. Knick-knacks of all kinds covered every available shelf and table as well as the fireplace mantle. (In back of the room was a half-opened door leading to an upstairs bedroom.)

"May as well show you the wardrobe. It's back in the 'catchall' as we call it, behind the kitchen. We have too much furniture, no room for this thing. So we thought of selling it," Mr. Cotter explained as he escorted us through a large neat looking kitchen from which a narrow staircase led to a floor above, perhaps the guest rooms and attic.

"Never had much use for the upstairs; don't like to

climb up there and we don't need it, either," he continued as he guided us to the "catchall", a structure adjoining the kitchen. And there it was, standing against the wall among lawn mowers, firewood and garden tools. It seemed to be an authentic Shaker made piece; though perhaps not one of the finest done by those superb craftsmen. With its generally simple design and white porcelain knobs, it looked like a typical Shaker piece such as we had seen in homes and museums. Designed for their monastic way of life, it was meant to be a one person wardrobe, combined with drawers and a larger space for hats or bonnets on one side. Only the cornice was missing, which gave it an incomplete, unfinished look.

"The top is somewhere upstairs in the attic. It came off and my wife kept it up there. She will find it for you and I can bring it to you sometime next week," he promised.

The asking price seemed reasonable. I looked at my wife who gave the needed nod of consent.

"Okay," I said, "we'll take it. We can load it right into the station wagon. I will bring it around to the back."

We paid for it in cash and Mr. Cotter made out a sales receipt. Then we drove off, pleased with our purchase. It was a practical piece of furniture, though not particularly attractive with the cornice missing. But Mr. Cotter had promised to bring it to us within a week. Two weeks went by and nothing happened. Then one late afternoon an old Dodge drove up to our house. From it a gray haired, skinny woman with gold rimmed glasses emerged.

"I am Mrs. Cotter," she announced as she stepped up to the front porch, "and I came here to take back the wardrobe. My husband had no business selling it to you. He is an old fool - stupid. I've changed my mind - don't want to sell that wardrobe."

It seemed that some form of an argument was about to

get going. We had bought it in good faith, held a legal receipt for it, and it was already full of our clothes in the master bedroom. In the end we did not part with our purchase though we never got the top for it either. And the skinny, spinsterish white haired lady, looking much older than her pudgy faced husband, drove off in a huff, and that was the end of it.

Last fall we invited a young couple for a cocktail on the lawn on a Sunday afternoon. We had met Jim and Alice many times at parties, and we liked them very much. They lived not too far from us in a neighboring village. We had driven past their neat looking house and spacious lawn many times. We were happy to be getting together with them at last at our hillside home. It had begun to get chilly outdoors, and we all moved into the house.

"We'll give you the tour," my wife suggested, "if you care to see our old house."

We took them from one room to another and finally got to the upper floor.

"Nice Shaker piece," Alice commented as she glanced into our bedroom from an upstairs hall door.

"It would be nicer if we had the missing cornice," I replied, "but it's been trouble enough as it is."

"Where did you get it?" Alice asked.

"Oh, years ago over at Neversville from some nutty pair, the Cotters, near the Methodist church."

"Isn't that a strange coincidence!" Alice exclaimed. "That's the house we lived in for 18 months when Jim got his job at the plant. We rented it from the estate. The Cotters died several years ago. What a place, what a place! We left it before our lease expired. It's a terrible place."

"What's so terrible about it?" I asked. "I remember it as a charming old house - only the people who lived there were a little odd."

"Well, I don't even want to talk about it," Alice continued. "Have you ever lived in a haunted house? You would not believe what we went through. I was miserable there the moment we moved in. Right from the beginning, I had a strange feeling that something was watching me every moment. It is hard to describe. I was there alone a good deal, with Jim at work and the children at school. I just couldn't understand it. You know, we were right in the center of the village. We were not as isolated as you are here. There were people walking by, driving by all day long. But the only place where I felt like myself was out on the lawn. The moment I went back into the house something was there with me. And then we had terrible dreams; Jim, the children too. Jim never had bad dreams before, and here we all had these terrible nightmares. We were floating, carried up into the air like balloons. It was not like flying in a plane or gliding like birds. We were floating up to the ceiling. Something told us to move towards the door, but in our dreams we were afraid that we might then float into the clouds. In the morning we all talked about it, day after day."

"It's hard to believe," I interrupted, "when you see the peaceful little village, the cozy clapboard house, and how charming it is with the dormer windows there in the shade of those great maples. It had all the markings of a very happy house."

"Happy house!" Alice protested, "I guess there are happy houses and unhappy houses. But this one really takes the prize!"

By now we all had settled around the fireplace in our living room.

"We may as well tell you the rest of our weird tale," Alice continued. "There was a second floor with dormer windows. Our daughter's bedroom used to be up there; she was about 17 then. It's that upper floor that really housed the spooks. There was a large closet. I wish I had one like it in our house now. But the closet was the lair of the spook. Whenever you opened the door it felt as if the cold tentacles of some octopus, some monster were about to touch you. I never went near it after a while. And then our 12 year old son really got the works. Whenever Charles went upstairs to get something, this black thing came out of the closet and hung on to his back. He came storming down the stairs to the kitchen, held on to the refrigerator and counted even numbers like: two-four-six-two-four-six. Then finally the black thing let him go and disappeared into thin air before we could see it. He must have heard about or read about counting these numbers but it seemed to exorcise the spell."

"We first thought that his imagination had gotten the better of him," Jim explained, "but it repeated itself time after time. So we had to accept it as the real thing. Charlie was not a timid boy. He was on all the teams in school. He was not afraid of anything. He went up again and again and always the black thing leaped on him from the big closet, and down he stormed counting those numbers, hanging on to the refrigerator. Even I didn't like to go upstairs unless I really had to, to locate a leak in the roof or something else that was important. So, after a year we had had it and found another place to rent before we bought our house. We are not a timid, superstitious family. None of us is psychic or did we ever before or after have any contact with the occult. But this place was really creepy."

"Well," I asked after a lengthy pause, "did someone else move into that house?"

"Yes," Jim replied, "the Everts took it. I don't think you know them. He is a retired Army man. Early retirement. They had no children. They had come here from abroad and had absolutely no way of knowing about the haunting."

"I think I met him once when I was invited to the local

gun club," I commented. "Yes, yes, he was a crack pistol shot there at the range. I remember watching him there once."

"They didn't stay long either," Jim continued. "Moved away before their lease expired. They avoided the upstairs rooms like the plague. There is nothing timid about the Everts, but they were very unhappy there. The Black Thing appeared to Mrs. Everts exactly as we experienced it. She is a vigorous, healthy woman in her fifties. When we heard her telling us about it, we were truly convinced that our Charlie was right and we were more than ever assured that our son had not been carried away by his imagination. You talk to them sometime. Their experiences match ours. They have a place now on Pine Hill Road."

"Someone lives there now? I asked.

"Yes," Alice replied, "the place was finally sold to an elderly couple. They seem to be very content there. We don't want to let them know what we went through. It wouldn't be fair to frighten them in their happy home. They never mentioned anything about spooks there to us. Perhaps the place has settled down by now and the Black Thing has moved away."

Ghosts, independent of time and space are sporadic and unpredictable. They come and they go.

CHAPTER 16

Merwin's Tombstone

Time and again I have stepped on Merwin's tombstone as I entered the charming home of our friends and neighbors, the Tuttles, for an hour or two of pleasant socializing. Later I learned the story about the macabre doorstep. It has recently been written up by Jeff Sommer for the *Knickerbocker News*, Albany, New York, and the material has been released to me for this book.

'ICHABOD CRANE' OF KINDERHOOK

Tucked away in the hills of Kinderhook is a white farmhouse built more than 160 years ago by a man named Jesse Merwin. A school teacher and, in prosperous middle-age, a gentleman farmer in this Columbia County town. Merwin is now unknown to most Americans.

But some literary historians and many residents of these Hudson Valley environs believe Jesse Merwin was the real life model for Ichabod Crane, the gaunt, ghost-ridden character chased by the Headless Horseman in Washington Irving's *Legend of Sleepy Hollow*.

Irving wrote early in his story that Sleepy Hollow is located near Tarry Town (now Tarrytown in Westchester County). But many experts believe the author derived inspiration from many places, including Kinderhook, where Irving paid an extended visit in 1809 and probably 1810. During that stay, Irving and Merwin became friends.

"In 1851, when the two were old men, Irving wrote Merwin a letter. On one side, Irving scribbled, 'Jesse Merwin - the original of Ichabod Crane,'" says Professor Andrew Myers, an Irving scholar at Fordham University. "I see no reason to doubt that Irving modeled Ichabod Crane after Merwin."

But Myers adds that "there was no one-to-one correspondence" between Merwin and the fictional character. No Headless Horseman rode after the real-life Ichabod Crane with a pumpkin head flung as a projectile. Nor was Merwin disappointed in love. Unlike Crane, who was spurned by the lovely Katrina Van Tassel, Merwin lived on to marry and build a home on a tranquil farm. Nourished by Irving's spectral tale, however, bizarre legends about Merwin and his descendants flourished in Kinderhook.

Merwin's farmhouse was sold out of his family more than 50 years ago to a retired plumber from Brooklyn, one Tom Flitcroft, according to the house's current owners. Esther L. and Franklin B. Tuttle, now a retired couple who also maintain an apartment in New York City, have inhabited the Merwin Farm for 35 years.

"A hundred years back, a kitchen was added to the house," Mrs. Tuttle says. "We put in heating and a telephone and did some remodeling. But otherwise it's much as it was in Merwin's time."

*Folklore and Tradition: The headless horseman rides again. . .
here in a play often produced by local amateur and camp groups.*

The farmhouse is different in one macabre respect, however. One unknown day late in the 19th century, someone removed the gravestones of Merwin and his wife from the Kinderhook cemetery. The marble slabs were carried to the Merwin farmhouse and left there, with their inscriptions turned face down. They were used as doorsteps. People have been walking on them ever since.

A lithe athletic woman who owns two horses and rides daily, Mrs. Tuttle was once a professional actress. She speaks with relish of her encounters with the Merwin legend. She and her family have lived with it amiably for more than three decades.

"People told us that if the tombstones were ever turned over, the Headless Horseman would ride again. That didn't bother us much. But we didn't touch the stones for many years," she says.

"One day in June about 20 years ago, a young man was working for us as a handyman. He was out front, near Jesse Merwin's tombstone, and happened to have a crowbar with him. I was curious. I wanted to know if Merwin's inscription was really on the bottom of the slab. So I told him to pry it up," she says.

She saw the inscription, satisfied herself that it was authentic, and replaced the tombstone. At first, it seemed that nothing happened.

"That night we took the children to New York for the weekend. My mother-in-law stayed here, though. She saw what happened. We used to have twin maple trees," she says, pointing to a spot in front of her house where only one maple now stands.

"A bolt of lightning struck the tree down the middle. It split the tree in half. My mother-in-law said she couldn't touch anything inside the house. The lightning bolt electrified everything," Mrs. Tuttle says.

She has never seen the Headless Horseman, but once thought she did.

"There's a road a couple of miles from here called Spook Rock Road," Mrs. Tuttle says. "I used to ride my horse there everyday. It's a good route, about 8 miles around. Seventeen years ago, I was riding with my daughter and a friend of hers. The girls were 13. It was late, and getting dark. It's a winding kind of road. We were talking.

"We reached a very dark spot. A black figure on a white horse suddenly appeared before us. Our horses reared back. They were terrified. So were we. We thought it was the Horseman. But it was my son Teddy. He liked to pull pranks like that."

Another son, Franklin James Tuttle, who is now an official at the National Commercial Bank in Albany, may have been visited by a Merwin ghost when Jimmy, as Mrs. Tuttle calls him, was still a child.

"We have a sleeping porch in the front," Mrs. Tuttle says. "The kids used to sleep there, but they said they didn't like it for some reason, so we moved them inside. My husband and I slept out there for years.

One day we were in the car, driving to New York, I think. We started talking about the porch. Little Jimmy had his thumb in his mouth. He removed his thumb and said, "I don't like the porch. I don't like the white mommy who wouldn't sing a song." And he put his thumb back in his mouth. We all sat up straight. Because we had never heard of any "white mommy." Jimmy wouldn't say anything else about her.

The Tuttles were mystified. But later, they began to hear tales of a descendant of Merwin, a lovely young girl named Nellie, who died of consumption.

"The family sent her away to the mountains for a cure," Mrs. Tuttle says. "But of course it didn't work. She came home. There are still some old-timers around who talk of beautiful Nellie Merwin. They say she had pale white skin and flaming red cheeks. The disease

might have done that. They say she slept out on the
porch for the fresh air. And she died on the porch 55 or
60 years ago. Some say she comes back now and then for
a visit."

As far as they know, the Tuttles have not been visited
by the Merwins or by the Headless Horseman for many
years. But the couple will not raise the tombstone of
Merwin or his wife again.

"I don't think we should take the risk," says Mr.
Tuttle, who was chairman of the board of the Atlantic
Mutual Insurance Co. until retiring 11 years ago. "I
don't think we can assume responsibility for releasing the
Headless Horseman."

CHAPTER 17

The Butler

Spring has been slow in coming, but it finally arrived in full glory, bathing the Grandma Moses-like countryside of Columbia County in comforting warm sunshine, encouraging buds and bulbs to burst.

Gordon and Wiggie Cox strolled about their lawn, which was soon to be shaded by the large sugar maples. Their distinguished house glistened in the bright midday sun.

"Sherry should be here any minute now; it's almost lunch time. Say - what do you think of having our cocktails outside?" Gordon suggested to his charming wife.

"Well, it's fine with me, but we haven't set up our lawn chairs . . . although we could sit right here on the slanting cellar door. It certainly is a most comfortable spot; we can just soak up the warm sunshine."

Soon Sherry's sporty black convertible pulled up across the road and parked in front of the large red hay barn facing the country lane. Sherry, a slim athletic looking Swede (his real name was Dr. Einar Sherndahl,

General Manager of the Winthrop Chemical Company*), was always on time for his appointments, especially for a luncheon invitation with his old friends and neighbors. Greeted by his hosts, he readily agreed with their suggestion of having cocktails on the sunny cellar door. Jacques, the butler, brought out three martinis on an engraved silver platter, a horseshow trophy.

They toasted the coming spring and enjoyed their first outdoor gathering of the year. Now and then, one could hear the neighing of horses from their boxstalls below the barn, or the baying of the pack of foxhounds in their kennel.

The Cox's were a horsey couple, dedicated to cross-country fox hunting. They were charter members of the local Foxhunt, serving as Masters of the Hunt for numerous terms. It was great hunt country, with gently rolling hills studded with dairy farms.

Soon Jacques served a second round of cocktails and asked what wine he should select in the cellar for lunch.

"Lucky you have this French couple," Sherry remarked, "a fine butler, and Michelle is a great cook. Hard to come by nowadays."

There seemed to be an unusually long lapse of time before the announcement that lunch was ready to be served. Wiggie was about to get up and see what caused the delay. Suddenly they heard a muffled shriek that came from below the slanted cellar door where Gordon's wine cellar was located. Inside the house a door banged, the front door opened and Michelle, waving her arms in mad excitement, stormed towards the party.

"Monsieur Cox, Madame Cox, un malheur horrible - venez, venez! Dans la cave, c'est Jacques! Il est mort. Il s'est pendu. Il s'est pendu. Lá bas d'un poutre dans la cave."

---

* The late Dr. Sherndahl had discovered Atropine, a substitute for Quinine. This was most important in our war effort when fighting in tropical countries.

Home of Mr. & Mrs. Gordon Cox.

"Michelle, pull yourself together and stop this French gibberish. Say it in English and make some sense." Gordon growled.

"Venez . . . come with me, quick - down in the cellar - Il est mort, Jacques - il s'est pendu from the beam, c'est horrible - il est mort."

Michelle led Gordon back into the house as Wiggie and Sherry followed, not quite comprehending what had happened down below in the cellar. Standing on top of the cellar stairs Gordon was first to face the grim tragedy. There, suspended from a heavy handhewn ceiling beam, a bunch of baling twine around his neck, was Jacques, the butler, who only a short time before had served the welcome drinks.

Gordon rushed down the steps staring in horror at the lifeless body hanging in front of him. From his vest pocket he pulled out his golden penknife, cutting through the tangled baling twine until finally the corpse dropped to the cellar floor. Now, joined by Sherry, tense, and horrified, he tried to establish any sign of life in the slumped body which stared at them with wide open eyes. Michelle, Jacques' wife, was being comforted by Wiggie.

"Il est mort," she wept, "Pourquoi - why has he done this to me?" she lamented. "What made him do it?"

Soon the entire household was in turmoil. A police car arrived, then an ambulance, and the coroner. The sunny spring day, the happy cocktail hour were forgotten as gloom and sorrow, sobs and tears took over. "Jacques est mort," but life had to go on though the memory of this tragic spring day was not soon forgotten.

Several years later Gordon told me that later on that fateful day he had walked down a farm lane and there he had thrown his cherished golden pen knife into a newly plowed field. He could not bear to keep the knife he had been forced to use in such tragic circumstances.

The event was never really forgotten Though the years

rolled by, the departed spirit of Jacques still hovered over the old country house. Strange mysterious phenomena began to be noticed. Doors would open and close in unexplained fashion, even on quiet windstill days and nights. Sometimes they would swing open slowly and close rapidly. Steps were heard on staircases and along the hallways leading to second floor bedrooms, often coming from the butler's quarters. However, no one was ever seen, no visual apparition ever occured. Then again for a long time none of the phenomena took place. They never ceased entirely but only happened if no more than one or two people were present in the house.

So the Coxes eventually got used to this, especially since no frightening visual manifestations took place. The spirit of the faithful butler roamed about at his volition, perhaps trying to carry out some unfinished job for his master.

Now many years have passed by and Gordon and Wiggie's son, Peter, lives with his wife and young daughter in his parents' former house. Following in the family tradition they are keeping a fine stable of hunters, and the kennel of foxhounds has been enlarged. Peter is Master of the Hunt as his father and mother had been. In the fall, when the leaves have turned color and the ripe cornstalks rustle in the breeze, the Old Chatham Hunt rides to the hounds over the picturesque autumn countryside.

The restless earthbound spirit of Jacques still haunts the household, which is now reaching toward a third generation. Little Ellenor, the youngest tenant of the mansion, follows enthusiastically in the tradition of the Cox family. She rides her white pony with skill and natural self confidence.

Only a few years ago when she was about four or five years old, the teenage son of friends and neighbors was asked to babysit while her parents attended a dinner party. Charlie had brought along some of his homework with good intentions of studying while enjoying the comfort of the Cox home. After a while he turned on the television set. Ellenor was peacefully asleep in her upstairs bedroom.

Suddenly a door banged somewhere in the large house. Charlie heard it but paid little attention to it until he heard footsteps along the upper hallway. Although he ruled out the possibility of an intruder, he decided to investigate and find out what this was all about. He went upstairs to check on his young charge, thinking she might perhaps have gotten up and walked along the hallway. But when he looked into the little girl's bedroom, Ellenor was sound asleep. Somewhat puzzled he returned to watch the TV show, when again the sound of firm footsteps - not at all the patter of a child - now came from the lower hall leading to the pantry. He turned off the TV and, really alarmed, rushed to the suspicious site. Charlie was not an easily frightened youngster. He was sturdy and well built for his age, active in many sports. His search ended without providing a logical explanation of the cause of the strange sounds.

As he was about to return to his TV program the door to the pantry flew wide open. He had closed it firmly just a minute before. All this made him uneasy and he hoped that his employers would soon return. It was now only about 10 P.M. and he had been told that his job might not end until midnight. He was now very alarmed and did not turn the TV on again. Things were not right here though they seemed peaceful and quiet again. Then it started all over again. The latch of the kitchen door rattled. The door opened wide and swung back, followed by solid footsteps in the direction of the butler's pantry. Now Charlie shuddered, he felt he could not cope with the situation alone any longer. He rushed to the phone and called his father.

"Someone's walking around in this house, Dad. I wish

you could come over and help find out what's going on here."

Soon he heard the comforting sound of car tires on the graveled drive. A car door slammed and his father appeared at the front door. Somewhat embarrassed Charlie told him about the strange goings-on and together they searched the house from cellar to attic and found nothing unusual.

They were still sitting in the library watching TV, with Ellenor sound asleep upstairs, when Charlie's employers returned from the party. Peter listened to the report and shrugged his shoulders.

"Well, I am sorry. It's all right, though," he explained, "we get this sometimes - not very often any more - but we think it is Jacques, Father's old butler, who hung himself down in the cellar 35 years ago. He still spooks around and gets a little noisy sometimes. But it's nothing to worry about. He's harmless and we're used to him."

Recently I called on Peter to check on the material for my story. He took me to the cellar steps from where his father's butler had jumped to his death into the baling twine noose. A small bunch of gray disintegrated twine still remains attached to the ceiling beam. Peter pointed to the wine cellar where Jacques was to select his last bottle of Medoc for his master's luncheon party.

CHAPTER 18

✑

Good Night

During all the years since I was married I rarely ever spent a night in my in-law's house. They lived in the suburbs in New Jersey. Their home could be reached by bus from New York and there had been no need for an overnight stay. A situation developed, however, that necessitated my presence there at an early morning hour and that made an overnight stop commendable.

I had rushed through a hasty supper. Rain and sleet were beating at our windows when I left our New York City apartment for my trip to the home of my in-laws. Leaving the protective comfort of the almost empty late-hour bus I faced the cold rain. Sleet spattered into my face and onto the slippery sidewalk that led to the house.

During the summer and fall, the sturdy stucco house was covered almost entirely by a lush growth of English ivy that gave it a charming and venerable character. Now the leafy cover had disappeared, and the small, gray house on the hillside had lost its inviting appearance as it came into view through the rain-streaked haze in the dim, cold glow of the street lights.

Answering my knock at the door, my father-in-law (Tom) greeted me and apologized for my having to come out to New Jersey on a night like this. I did not mind the journey, as long as I could be of some use to the aging couple. Tom had to go to the hospital for some outpatient treatment of a serious ailment very early in the morning and some good neighbor had offered to drive him there.

His wife could not be left alone in the house. She had become forgetful and was no longer fully responsible or able to function alone in the household. She might forget to turn off water faucets or the gas stove. All was well because Tom always looked after such matters. But in the early morning he would have to leave, and I was to be in charge of the house during his absence.

Tom made me a glass of hot tea flavored with some Jamaican rum. This was a real treat after my facing the unfriendly elements of the outside and it also served as a soothing nightcap.

I was offered "Paul's room" for my sleeping quarters. I rarely ever had been in this small bedroom-sitting room, which had been occupied by my wife's bachelor uncle until his death a few years ago. Paul had been a quiet, unassuming person and his life had been uneventful. He had worked hard all the years before his retirement. Now, he was gone. His room had been left unchanged and of no special use.

I had become drowsy at this point after the comforting tea and rum, and I was ready for a good night's sleep. The room had a musty smell, as unused places acquire, aided by the humidity of the atmosphere. I hung my clothes in the spacious, empty closet, turned on the bed-side light before slipping between the fresh sheets. When I turned off the light after a short period of reading the evening paper, the house was engulfed in peaceful tranquility. I don't remember how long I had dozed or slept when I was awakened by some strange sounds right under my bed. I decided to ignore it, as I was too tired to be bothered. It must have been well past midnight when I was awakened again by some more pronounced rumpus below the bed. This time I thought it advisable to investigate. I turned on the bedside table lamp, got out from under my comfortable covers to find myself on hands and knees looking under the bedstead. There was nothing to be found except my wet shoes. Somewhat annoyed by my own seemingly unnecessary investigation I soon dropped off into sound sleep again, while the entire house was in a state of peaceful slumber.

It is hard to say how long I must have been sleeping when I was awakened, this time by a much more vigorous racket under the bed. I listened as it increased until it resembled the sound of some good sized animals fighting right under my bed. It had to be stopped and its cause had to be established. It was too disturbing and eerie to be ignored. As I jumped out of bed the weird sounds ceased. Again I looked under the bed where the noises had centered. I even investigated the barren closet. The radiator under the window was cold, leaving the room temperature rather chilly. I went back to bed, frustrated by the interruptions of my sleep in this otherwise quiet and peaceful house. I felt rather foolish, exhausted and sufficiently tired to give in to whatever this could have been. After all, I occasionally had been exposed to poltergeists at our old farmhouse in the Berkshires. We had learned to accept them, gotten used to them if and when they made their sporadic appearances.

When I woke up the next morning, the rain had stopped and the sun was beginning to send its rays through the window curtains. I went downstairs, where I found the small kitchen table all prepared for my breakfast. Before leaving for the hospital the kind old man had put everything in readiness. He always was a thoughtful, considerate person and a gracious host.

While I enjoyed my morning coffee and after breakfast pipe the events of the restless night occupied my mind. Could the rumpus under the bed have been induced by a poltergeist, by some non-corporeal personal agency? Was it, perhaps, the spirit of the bachelor uncle who resented my sleeping in his small sanctuary? He often had been critical of me since his pace of life was way out of step with ours. He might have feared that I would take over his former abode and therefore shown his resentment.

When Tom returned from the hospital a few hours later I soon set out on my return trip to New York without a mention of my nocturnal experience. I did not hesitate, however, to report my weird adventure to my wife. She acknowledged that she also had heard strange noises while recently staying over at her parents' house.

"I remember it seemed as if someone was rummaging in the hallway linen closet, and when I set out to investigate, everyone in the house was sound asleep. You know," she said after a pause, "at one time Paul's room had been my grandfather's room. He had died there 30 years ago. He had been rather dominating, the undisputed master of his house. I don't think that you would have liked him - and he may have felt the same about you. If some poltergeist had been the cause of your adventure at my parent's home I would not have been surprised if the spirit of my grandfather had something to do with it. He could be quite forceful while he was still alive."

Within a relatively short time Tom succumbed to his ailment. Soon after his wife died. The sturdy ivy covered house was sold and the new owners made drastic changes, renovating the old family home.

I am inclined to believe that the changed environment would discourage any earthbound spirits - confused in a timeless world - and make them lose interest and not maintain any further desire to participate in our worldly sphere.

CHAPTER 19

✍

The Chair Factory

We met the MacDonalds at a small, informal dinner party on the banks of nearby Queechy Lake in Canaan, New York. They were a charming young couple who owned a house in the neighboring township of Lebanon. Donald MacDonald, an athletic young Scotsman in his late twenties, had a stocky build and a ruddy outdoors complexion. He would probably look very good wearing his native kilt. Louise, his wife, was a beautiful young woman, with blond hair framing her delicate, heart-shaped face. Her slender figure was perfect for fashion modeling. In fact, she functions as a model, showing the family business products - Scottish-made, sheepskin coats - and her pictures appear regularly in national advertising. Donald conducts his business from Mount Lebanon, where their home, office and warehouse are located.

Our host, also a Scotsman but of American lineage, led the conversation to our house, suggesting that the young couple come and see our place.

"It's a great old farmhouse on a hillside overlooking

the Hudson Valley," he explained, "and it's complete with a ghost, as every old house should be."

"Sounds great!" Louise turned to us. "In fact, that ghost part is right up our alley. We have a spook or two at our old Shaker building, pretty lively at times. We must get together and compare notes."

It was a pleasure listening to her clear voice, her cultured English with barely a trace of a Scottish accent. Nothing seemed more inviting than an early get-together with this attractive couple. Within a short time we saw them again, when they came to a cocktail party on the lawn at our place, and again on a visit to their place.

It was a beautiful, balmy day when we drove over. The last time we had been in the Shaker settlement had been about 25 years earlier. At that time, we had met the few surviving members of the sect, and I had taken a number of pictures of the aging sisters, who lived in an almost deserted four-storey building. We had taken our two-year old son along. As we talked to ninety-year-old Eldress Sarah Collins, she looked at our son in his mother's arms.

"Yes," she said, chuckling in her old woman's voice, "we Shakers made everything up here - except babies!"

A religious sect that was based on communal living, the Shakers were nevertheless celibates; perhaps this is one of the reasons why their religious beliefs, their fine art, their famous craftsmanship finally died out. Today their heritage is admired in museums and among collectors all over the country.

As we drove along Shaker Hill Road, we passed the site where years ago I had met and photographed the last of the Mount Lebanon Shakers. The large four-storey clapboard building had been torn down, though many of the fine structures are still standing. Several are being used to house a prep school, the Darrow School. Almost at the end of the road we saw the long, white picket fence

Eldress Sarah, 92 years of age.

Eldress Sarah informing us that they made everything at their Mt. Lebanon settlement but babies.

Hands of Sister Rosetta.

Sister Rosetta who wrote poetry and music.

Shaker barn.

where we turned into the semicircular driveway. We stopped at the columned entrance to the stone house and were greeted by the MacDonalds. They led us through a wide hallway decorated with a fine collection of paintings. We went down a stairway leading to the lower floor, which in most houses would be the cellar. Since the building sits on a sloping hillside, the lower floor was used for a dining room, kitchen and pantry.

The hall opened up to a porch, with flower baskets and birdfeeders suspended from the ceiling. A few steps lower we came to a wide terrace, and here we settled down in comfortable lounge chairs. From here, a magnificent view stretched out over miles of fields and pastures in the idyllic Lebanon Valley. A picturesque pond below the house, where ducks, geese and swans enjoyed the warmth of the afternoon sun, added to the enchanting vista.

The three-storey house, topped by an attic with dormer windows, was built of fieldstone and had the air of an English country mansion. It had no resemblance to the austere style of the other Shaker buildings.

"We loved this place the moment we saw it," our hosts informed us. "Those old Shakers knew how to select a perfect spot for their settlement when they started their community at the end of the eighteenth century here in the foothills of the Berkshires. Our house had been their chair factory."

"Some chair factory!" I replied, admiring the aristocratic, solid looking structure."

Enchanted by this scenery and basking in the late afternoon sunlight, we soon learned more from our host, as birds darted over our heads toward the feeders and tiny hummingbirds dove into the red and blue petunia blossoms in the hanging flower baskets.

Their lovely home had indeed been a chair factory. Here the industrious Shakers had made their exquisite furniture, especially the famous Shaker chairs, which were sold to "the world," as the sect referred to people outside of their domain. When the industrial revolution gained momentum it finally struck the death blow to the products of superb quality craftsmanship. Their industry collapsed, eventually leading to the end of the once flourishing community.

"This may perhaps be the reason why the old Shakers are haunting us. It's their resentment of the *modern age*," Donald explained, as he refilled our glasses.

When the settlement was finally abandoned, the empty, neglected buildings, deprived of repair, were in danger of disintegration and final collapse. Some other purpose had to be found for their use. The Darrow School was established, and the old chair factory was bought by the Robertsons. They were the owners of the well known cosmetic firm, Mary Chess. They renovated the barren, empty stone building in grand style and with excellent taste. Their property included a large clapboard building that once served as the living quarters of the Shaker workers. Dismantling the neglected structure, they transferred its fine interior woodwork and refitted it on the barren walls of the former chair factory. Now the wall paneling, window casings and closets are tastefully installed in the restored house. Eventually, after about 20 years, it was for sale again and the MacDonalds moved into this beautiful, luxurious manor house. An adjoining large, barn-like structure, once the warehouse for Shaker craft products, now serves the MacDonald enterprise as the shipping center for their import products.

"I had dreamt about this house years ago when I went to boarding school in Scotland." Louise informed us. "I saw it many times in my dreams. When we came here to buy the place it seemed as if I had been here before. Every detail was familiar to me; the long white picket fence, the wide hallways, the wood paneled rooms, even the terrace with its lovely view over the valley. It was a strange feeling to have a dream become reality."

"It was not so long ago," I said, "that you attended that school in Scotland. Did you like it there?"

"Oh yes, indeed. The school was a wonderful place, It's a very old school and at one time it had been a residence of Mary, Queen of Scots. The ancient stone house where she had stayed is now used as the school library. The upstairs bedroom is still as it was in Queen Mary's day, with her bed recessed in an alcove. It's a spooky place - haunted. We girls never went alone to that library. Strange things happened there."

"Did you see the Queen's ghost?" I interrupted.

"No, I never did see her ghost. But many times girls walking up or down that staircase were kicked and pushed by unexplained forces. Some were even hurt falling down the stairs. It was so bad that the headmistress had the place exorcised, but that did not help very much."

"Scotland, I suppose, has many haunted places and when you came here you were somewhat tolerant of strange goings on, weren't you?" I asked.

"Well, we Scotch have learned to live with ghosts, I suppose. That library had been a private residence before the school bought it. A family had been living there with their son. We heard that the boy, perhaps about 12 years old at that time, had seen a strange apparition at the garden gate in bright daylight . . . a man in medieval attire, wearing a brown robe almost like a monk's but not cut the way a monk's robe is. He reported this strange encounter to his parents. But nothing more happened and the incident was forgotten. Years later, when as a young man, he visited the British museum in London he saw a painting of Lord Darnley, a husband of Mary, Queen of Scots. It was the perfect image of what he had seen coming through the gate of their former house. So you can see the old school library was a haunty place and we girls were more than aware of it."

It was a pleasure listening to the lovely voice of this beautiful Scottish lassie, hearing the eerie tale told here in this cheerful setting on the terrace of their elegant home as the late afternoon sun was descending toward the horizon. Louise continued.

"When we first moved in here soon after our wedding and an extensive honeymoon in Africa, I was rather homesick for Scotland and I missed my old friends. But the place is so beautiful and now we are very happy here and we have many new friends. We moved to this house three years ago in May. The summer was lovely here, but come fall this cheerful place changed its images. We were being haunted."

"You can learn to live with ghosts," I explained, "especially if it's a benevolent ghost like ours."

"Yes, I agree," our host replied, "but I don't think our ghosts can be termed benevolent. They make us rather uncomfortable at times. I am away on business occasionally and it's been rough on Louise, though she is a brave girl. Now, it's getting chilly out here and we must take you around in the house and tell you more about it."

As we entered the house we were shown the large elegant wood paneled dining room, furnished with a large Shaker dining table and Shaker ladder back chairs. Crossing the hall we saw the spacious modern kitchen and pantry adjoining the nursery. Here we met their baby son, attended by a baby sitter. Louise picked up her young son, cheerfully smiling and happy in his mother's arms.

"Once the baby arrived our haunting seemed to have stopped," Louise commented, "and that was an additional blessing."

We ascended the stairs to the second floor and entered a large living room, which like the rest of the premises was covered with wood paneling from the demolished building across the road. This sets off the windows, which are recessed deeply in the thick stone walls. The fireplace was paneled in the same manner. There was an equally large library done in the same style, enhanced by Donald's collection of fine paintings and many fine pieces of Shaker made furniture. Finally we were shown the bedrooms on the third floor, where most of the "haunting" had taken place.

"It's here in our bedroom," Donald explained, "that our ghostly friends really carried on in a big way. It all started during the fall of our first year, after a blissful summer here. The Robertsons had done a great job making it a fine place to live in. We could not have found a more pleasant and suitable spot. There's a good size house and an equally spacious storage building, perfect for our shipping center."

"We were not too upset at first when we were awakened during the night, and, occasionally at almost any hour of the day, by footsteps on the staircases and along the halls. There was pounding and hammering and what may be the sound of turning wheels. You know we Scotch are a hardy sort and a little haunting is quite acceptable to most of us."

"But then it really began," Louise chimed in. "Door latches would rattle and wake us up during the night. Well, Donald has a fine collection of sporting guns and an intruder would have met a rough welcome. But there was no one. It seemed as though someone wanted to get into the bedroom. But there was nobody except the two of us in this large room."

"Then, one night after some strange sounds this picture fell off the wall." Donald pointed to one of the Japanese oriental prints arranged in a group between the windows on the west wall.

"It fell off the wall, the frame was broken and glass

scattered on the floor, though the solid nail and the picture were intact. It seemed as if it had been pushed away from the wall by some unexplained force. This happened several times, always about 1:30 A.M. It was always the same picture though I had firmly glued it together. I am a pretty competent repairman." Donald smiled with self confidence. "What I glue together holds. I cannot possibly ascribe this to natural causes."

"Finally one night the restless spirits appeared in our bedroom. We had been sound asleep when we were awakened again by the rattling of the thumb latch of this door on the left. The door never opened, but an eerie apparition, a woman wearing a long dark cape, entered through the closed doors. She walked slowly along the wall and soon disappeared through the closed door at the other end of the bedroom. An ice cold chill permeated the entire bedroom. We were both wide awake, gazing at this performance, but we could not speak. This time we were truly frightened. It was exactly 1:30 A.M. again when we turned on the lights and looked at the clock. We were too shaken to fall asleep again and so we went downstairs to have a cup of strong tea in the kitchen. We were chilled, shivering and upset. The following night nothing happened and we tried to forget the entire matter. However, a week or so later the same thing repeated itself. The same apparition, the woman in the black cape, wandered in from the same door and disappeared as before through the closed door at the other corner of the room."

"I guess this is not something one can get used to, no matter how brave you are or how much you try to convince yourself that there are no such things as ghosts," I commented on the eerie tale.

"We admit," Donald assured us, "that we were frightened - momentarily paralyzed - and we did not know what might happen next. We even considered leaving our bedroom and sleeping in the guest room across the hall.

*Door of master bedroom where ghostly apparitions enter -
always at 1:30 A.M.*

Shaker living quarters: North Family building. It had an early form of central heating and an efficient water cooling system in the basement. It was demolished as a fire hazard in 1973.

*The MacDonald residence that once had been
the Shaker Chair Factory.*

"Then one night I was awakened again, and I couldn't believe my eyes. There, through the same door, the figure of a man appeared. He was bearded. That's all I could see of his face. He wore period clothes that could perhaps be called Victorian or Edwardian. A long Prince Albert coat is the nearest I can come to describing it. He slowly walked toward our bed, on the side where Louise was sleeping. He sat down at the bedside and took hold of Louise's hand in a manner a doctor might do to take the pulse of a patient. I was absolutely petrified. I could only stare at the apparition. I could not move a muscle. He sat there for perhaps a few minutes - time is hard to judge under such conditions - then he got up again, walked toward the door and there the apparition disappeared before reaching the door.

"I turned on the light. Louise was sound asleep. A cold chill again swept through the room and it was exactly 1:30 A.M.

"The next morning we decided to surrender our bedroom to the ghostly night visitors. From that night on we slept in the guest room across the hall. It was not until early spring that we gathered enough courage to return to our large sunny master bedroom again."

"Donald does not take defeat without a fight," Louise continued. "We loved the great old house. It's so perfect for us with the warehouse and so well located with Pittsfield only a few miles away. We were not very happy for awhile, but we would not surrender to the phantoms. During the spring and summer months the spirits left us alone and it seemed when the baby arrived all strange goings on ceased."

Could it have been resentment or even fear of the presence of a baby in the house that halted the haunting? This and other questions remain unanswered. Why would some restless spirits haunt this young Scottish couple in their happy new home? Haunting is usually traceable to guilt, resentment, unfinished business, sometimes an attachment to people or places. It seems believable that spirits of the Shakers felt great bitterness at seeing their flourishing "adventure" (as it is often referred to in Shaker literature) falling apart, defeated and finally destroyed. Their Chair Factory, the temple of their fine craftsmanship, had been taken over by the worldly people. Their former living quarters had been demolished and in part used to transform their chaste workshop into a beautiful manor house. Perhaps they returned, turning the clock back, wanting to relive the times of their Shaker Eden at Mount Lebanon.

CHAPTER 20

⌒

Apple Blossoms

Spring had arrived in full force, and nothing was more welcome to me than Peter and Joan's invitation to spend the weekend at their lovely home in New Jersey. It was already late Saturday afternoon when I stepped off the train, since I had not been able to leave my New York City studio any earlier in the day. Peter met me at the railroad station and drove me through the budding, blooming countryside to their house. Everywhere the lawns looked fresh and green, studded with colorful tulip beds. Apple trees bloomed in gardens and orchards.

Their home was surrounded by well kept lawns and flower beds where tulips, hyacinths and narcissus were at the height of their glory, some of them right underneath white blooming apple trees. Joan, a tall, athletic New Englander, greeted me at the door, where she introduced me to their other weekend guest, Jim Collins. He was a young clerk at Peter's plant, a copper smelter and refinery in the nearby coastal area. Peter, a brilliant engineer, was general manager of the plant. He and I were fraternity brothers, though he was perhaps eight or ten years my senior at the university.

It was warm enough for us to gather on their porch for a welcome drink and enjoy a perfect spring day in the great outdoors. Jim was about my age, perhaps a few inches taller, with brown eyes and dark brown hair. He was what may be called an artistic type, although it was I who was earning a living in the arts, while Jim worked in the office of Peter's noisy metallurgical plant. Soon our hosts brought up the subject of plans for Sunday. We were to drive over to a stable a few miles away to go riding in the open country. The couple loved horses and had recently bought a new horse which they were eager to show me. I had anticipated such a project and had brought along my riding gear. Nothing appealed to me more than the prospect of a good run in the refreshing countryside, and I was eager to admire their new pride and joy.

Jim's reaction to the plan was rather negative. While he loved country living, horseback riding did not appeal to him. He stated that he would prefer to stay at home on Sunday and enjoy the peaceful quiet of the garden. "Let me sit here among the beautiful flowers under the magnificent apple blossoms."

Off we went the next morning to the stables. The new horse was a beautiful chestnut Morgan, perhaps seventeen hands high. Peter was a good match for his steed. He was tall, blond and blue-eyed, with great enthusiasm for outdoor activities. Jean's horse was a black Arabian, a handsome creature with an arched neck and a great deal of spirit. A sturdy gray mare of the American saddle horse type was assigned to me. We got along well on our outing along well kept bridlepaths in the flat agricultural landscape. At one point my steed gave me quite a surprise. We flushed a cock pheasant from the bushy roadside fence. The mare shied, reared and nearly threw me into the bushes. But outside of this little incident, we remained on good terms, and I had no trouble keeping up with my hosts, even though they were both much better riders than I was.

We arrived home about lunchtime, ready for a good cocktail to settle us down to a pedestrian world. The homecoming, however, was not very joyous. Jim met us at the door smiling from ear to ear, obviously pleased with himself. "Come in and see what I have done," he said, but as soon as Joan entered the house there was a loud outburst.

"Terrible! Terrible! Take it away! Quick!" she shouted. "This is terrible! It's bad luck - worse! This is terrible."

As we followed Joan indoors we saw what had given her such a shock. Jim had decorated the entire house with flowering branches from the apple trees. Every vase was filled. The flowers were on bureaus, side tables, coffee tables; everywhere there were apple blossoms.

"Take this stuff out - all of it - right away!" Joan shuddered as she slumped into an armchair, her face in tears. "Those blossoms," she stammered, "they are bad luck. They mean Death!"

Peter and I looked at each other in somber surprise. We just could not comprehend the significance of this hysterical outburst. Jim stood at the door, downcast, like a beaten dog. He, too, could not understand the meaning of this emotional reaction. He had wanted to please his hostess with a great flowering homecoming. He had meant so well, and now he was perplexed and sad.

"Take it all out! I cannot stand it any longer! Please!" Joan begged, hunched in an armchair. We followed her orders in silent obedience, still not comprehending the meaning of her depression.

"Silly, superstitious nonsense!" Peter grunted as we three carried the lovely blossoms to the compost heap in the back of the garden.

When we finally settled down to have lunch, Joan tried to explain to us the cause of her outburst.

"My mother, and my grandmother, too, would never allow apple blossoms in our house. It was a strict taboo. I have heard many grim, horrifying tales of the consequences. Believe me, this is no silly superstition."

We did not want to hear any more about this, and the subject was dropped to save the day. Later on, however, in talking to my host on the sunny porch, the upsetting matter came up again.

"Perhaps all this stems back to pagan times," I commented, "back to the days of Wotan and Thor and all the Anglo-Saxon gods." We both were well versed in classical and Nordic mythology.

"There was Ostoera (Eostre), the goddess of spring," I continued. "Our Christian Easter is named for this pagan deity. When Christianity was brought into Europe by the ancient monks, they could not eradicate this pagan religion all of a sudden. So even today, we still have our calendar full of names of pagan gods: Tuesday, *Zeus Day*; Wednesday, *Wotan's Day*; Thursday, *Thor's Day*; and Friday named for Freyia, the Saxon goddess of love. Some of our months are named after old deities as well. March is named for Mars, the Roman god of war, and June is named after Juno, the queen of the gods, and so it goes. This ancient belief did not die out all of a sudden. It survived (the *Goetterdaemmerung*), the 'twilight of the gods,' and it still lingers around."

Peter agreed with me, and he added to my explanation. "Perhaps those old heathens 'decked the halls with boughs of holly' at Christmas and with boughs of apple blossoms in the springtime. Apple blossoms might have been brought to Eostre's altar to stay in the good graces of their beautiful young goddess.

The Christian monks condemned all this behavior and called it devil worship and witchcraft that would bring bad luck to those who worshipped or even remembered those ancient gods. And that's why we have these superstitions."

"That's exactly it," I agreed. "We are stuck with crazy superstitions dating back almost two thousand years! Well, let's drop this subject and enjoy this great spring day."

Later in the evening, my hosts drove me back to the station. Jim stayed over another night and Peter was to take him back to the plant the next morning. At noontime Monday, in my New York studio, I answered the phone. It was Joan calling with an emotional tone of voice. "I have some shocking news for you. We found Jim *dead* in his room this morning." I gasped as she continued, "This nice young fellow was never sick a day in his life!"

Joan's grim message seemed almost incredible. I was stunned. My mind raced back to my conversation with Peter, to Joan's shocking reaction to the apple blossoms in her house. One question came to me, and I have never been able to answer it. Was there something to the old superstition after all? Every spring, when the apple blossoms are in bloom, I remember this tragic event that happened many years ago.

CHAPTER 21

The Seer

We had arrived for the weekend at the end of a long journey from the city. Touches of early fall were in evidence everywhere. Some branches of maples had already changed the color of their leaves to red and yellow. Fall flowers were swaying in the gentle breeze at the roadside; goldenrod, Queen Anne's lace and wild asters, and large stretches of purple blooms covered the swampy areas. Our old farmhouse looked snug and inviting in the shade of tall elms under a blue sky.

As we turned the key in the front door the phone rang. I dropped my suitcase and answered the call.

"I am Mrs. Jones," a young woman's voice addressed me, "and I read your interesting piece about your haunted house in *Fate* magazine. We, that is myself and two friends, would like to see your place if we may. Would you let us drop by for just a short visit?"

"Well, of course, you can," I answered, somewhat flattered by the favorable comment from a reader of my story, "When would you like to come by?"

"Sunday, perhaps about noon. That would be the most

convenient for us. We are not very far from there. We are so grateful that you will allow us to meet you and see your house."

I reported the phone call to my wife Ruth who immediately took a dim view of the matter.

"You should not have asked them. Most likely the woman you spoke to is a newspaper reporter who wants to write about our place for some paper. We don't want any more local publicity about our haunted house."

Perhaps she was right, but I had issued the invitation and there was nothing more to be done about it.

Promptly at noon the following day a dark green sedan with a Florida license plate drove up to the house and three people emerged, two younger women in their thirties and one a generation older, perhaps the mother of one of the two. After a brief introduction I escorted our guests to the comfortable lawn chairs in the shade of the elms. After some complimentary remarks about our place and the view towards the Hudson Valley, the young woman who had made the phone call explained to us that the older woman was indeed her mother. The other was her friend who had driven up with her from her home in Florida to visit her parents in nearby Hayt Corners for a week or two.

"My friend's name is Penny Thorne . . . glad to get away from the Florida summer for awhile. Penny has not seen or read your story, but she is very interested in psychic matters. An ordained minister who not only studied parapsychology, she is also a gifted psychic who can, under the right circumstances, see into the past. We were curious to find out if she could tell us something about your house."

The Reverend Penny Thorne, an attractive brunette, looking chic in her well tailored tweed suit, nodded her approval.

"I feel this house has something interesting to offer."

My wife, relieved that we were not dealing with newspaper reporters, put on her best hostess smile. Curious about our visitor, she led the party toward the house for a tour of the premises.

As soon as we had entered the central hall and turned into the dining room to the right, Penny Thorne announced in a casual, conversational manner, "I see a young woman dressed in a simple garb as may have been worn by members of a religious sect. She is bent over an ironing board, obviously not happy about her task. She is struggling, about to iron some stiff material . . . perhaps in the shape of a starched bonnet. She is young and frail and looks rather tired."

Astonished by the statement, my wife and I exchanged glances of surprise. Nothing of this had been mentioned in my article. However, in a book of poems and letters, written by our Quaker maiden, "ghost," Mary Mehitable Chase, she mentioned in one of her letters that she often called on an old couple at a nearby cottage. There she gave a helping hand to the old woman with her household tasks. In her letters she once referred to the difficulty she had in ironing her Quaker bonnets, obviously a tedious task for her.

We now opened the door to enter the former summer kitchen, the only unfinished part of the house. It had been left as we found it with peeling, stained wallpaper that also covered the uneven ceiling. We used it as a rough workshop and for storing garden tools and firewood. At the far side a door led to what once had been a pantry. The right panel of the door is marked by the grim pattern of a shotgun blast. Pellets of the shot are still imbedded in the surrounding woodwork. The people who owned our house before us - according to reports from neighbors - had shot at the "ghost" that had frightened and haunted them. Not long after this they left in a great hurry and placed the farm on the real estate market. We did not mention this to the Reverend, nor did we point out the pattern of the gun blast in the door panel to her. To our surprise she did not seem interested in this un-friendly and depressing section of the house.

We returned to the central hall, gave a brief glance at the living room and then proceeded up the stairs to our four bedrooms. Our guests admired our simple furnish-ings, the brightness and cheerfulness of the rooms and the general decorations. Penny lingered at the smallest of the four rooms, which we called the yellow room. We had painted the walls a bright lemon with white woodwork. For a minute she looked at the large four poster bed that took up a great deal of space in the small but cheerful bedroom.

"I see a little boy sleeping in this bed. He is perhaps 8 or 9 years old and has dark hair and big brown eyes. But . . . ," and she hesitated for a second in her casual way of speech, "he died some years ago."

A chill went through us as we heard her last words. Indeed this room had always been the bedroom for one of our son's young friends and playmates, Jimmy. He had been our guest often and for weeks at a time. The two youngsters loved to be at our farm in the summer where they romped and played, setting up wigwams on the lawn or building tree houses. They had been great friends un-til some years later when tragedy struck. Jimmy had died - a case of terminal cancer - when he was a freshman at college at the age of 19.

How could Penny know this and see the little boy in this small, cheerful room? Only Ruth and I knew about this tragedy. Shocked by the words of the seer, we all proceeded silently down the staircase to our spacious living room on the first floor.

Refusing our offer of tea or any other refreshments, our guests settled in the comfortable chairs and sofa in front of the fireplace, not in use on this lovely, mild

September day.

In her casual conversational tone, never going into a trance or silent meditation, Penny told us that this had been more than one room and that the northwest section had once been a small bedroom. When we renovated part of the house we had removed the partitions of two small rooms. The outside walls had been insulated and replastered. Our guest again admired the large cheerful room, our simple Early American furniture, the old organ, tables and paintings. As the conversation flowed Penny came up with another startling comment.

"I see an old woman lying on a narrow four poster bed there in the northwest corner. She is not a happy person, perhaps ailing. She is cantankerous and demanding toward the two young women who are trying to help her."

Again her vision seemed convincing to us. In Mary Chases's book the young Quaker poet refers to her aging mother, walking with a cane and suffering from some ailment. She seldom speaks of her, only of her father whom she admired and loved. It seemed most likely that a downstairs bedroom had been convenient for an ailing person who might have difficulties climbing the stairs. Therefore, a room with a window to the west, the best view from the house, would have been the perfect place for an ailing old mother.

Ruth was sitting in an old upholstered Edwardian chair enjoying the casual, flowing conversation and the fascinating comments when Penny spoke again.

"I see a dog, a rather large dog - white with black dotted markings all over his furry coat. He is a very noble dog, perhaps has won prizes in shows. And now he's putting his paw on Mrs. von Behr's arm that is resting on the green upholstered arm of the chair."

A chill ran through Ruth's spine as she listened to the seer's comment. Indeed we had a dog, named Dash, a registered English setter. He had not won prizes as Penny had told us, but he was truly a noble dog, a great hunter and a loving pet. A year or two later I wrote a story about him that was published in *Outdoor Life* and reprinted in "The Best Sports Stories of 1974." So often had he placed his furry paw on Ruth's or my arm as we sat in the squeaky old rocking chair, looking at us with his pleading brown eyes.

This casual comment of Penny's really shook my wife as she was very attached to Dash. He had died years ago at the age of 16, a great and noble dog to his last days.

"This house has an interesting and lively past," Penny pointed out. "I still see some more activity here, even black people are about, but I cannot get a clear vision of what they are all doing."

Our house, having been a farm and also for a time a small boarding school under the leadership of Thurston Chase, Mary's father, must have always been a bustling center of activity. In her book, Mary talks about "the African women" who worked at the place. They were not slaves, as Quakers did not have slaves, but they employed some African women in their large and busy household.

Penny's face had become somewhat pensive, her appealing smile had faded away as she spoke again.

"Perhaps I should not mention it to you," and again she hesitated, "I see somewhere a murder."

A deep silence had fallen over our gathering.

"I cannot localize it - but there is somewhere - a murder. A premeditated murder, but my vision is not clear."

We all gasped. This is the first time Penny's casual way had ceased. She seemed pensive and tense.

"There has never been a murder in this house," I replied, "and we are pretty well informed about the past of our old farm."

"I see it though. I cannot localize it, but I am sure

about a murder," Penny persisted, "it may not even have occurred right here, but it took place."

We shook our heads and felt for the first time during this fascinating visit that our seer had gone astray. Suddenly it dawned on me.

"Ruth," I said after a long, and painful pause, "perhaps there is a connection."

We know from archives of the nearby Quaker Meeting House that at one time Thurston Chase had employed a young teacher at his school, a Phineas Gurley. He later became a minister. (In one of her published letters Mary Chase begged him not to become a minster because Quakers did not believe in paid clergy. And in one of her poems, the only one motivated by romantic love, she seems to be inspired by this young man . . . perhaps the only great romance in her short life.) As time went on Phineas Gurley entered the ministry and later had become Abraham Lincoln's minister. After the assassination he sat at the bedside of the dying president and he also conducted the funeral service. When I mentioned this to our Reverend Penny Thorne she confirmed this as the murder she had envisioned - far away, though connected with this house through the young teacher. So Penny's last and most shocking statement had been confirmed.

Soon after this our guests were ready to depart. As we led them to their car we thanked Penny for her fascinating revelations.

"You certainly have proven to us, in your easy and yet most convincing manner, that you can see into the past of our old house. Will you perhaps grant me one more question," I said as we shook hands. "Are you, may I ask, also able to see into the future?"

"I could," she replied. "But," and she hesitated, "I never will. It is not good to unveil the future."

ACKNOWLEDGEMENTS

Years of searching and the kind cooperation of friends, neighbors and benevolent publishers have brought this book together. I am deeply indebted to all and am listing those who contributed written material as well as those who provided me with valuable information.

I wrote my first ghost stories, now Chapters 1 and 9 in this book, several years ago. Chapter 1 was published in August 1972 in condensed form and Chapter 9 in August 1976, both of them by *Fate* Magazine, Clark Publishing Co., 500 Hyacinth Place, Highland Park, Illinois.

Material for Chapters 5, 6 and 7 had been published by *The Chatham Courier*, Chatham, New York, and turned over to me by its president, Albert Callan.

Chapter 10 was written in German by His Royal Highness, Prince Ernst Heinrich von Sachsen and published by List Verlag, Munich, West Germany in *My Life: From Royal Palace to Farm Cottage*. Chapter 11 was also written by His Royal Highness but has not previously been published. It was later contributed through the kindness of the Prince's widow, Her Royal Highness, Princess Virginia von Sachsen. These Chapters have been translated by me.

Chapter 17 was written by Jeff Sommer, *The Knickerbocker News*, Albany, New York, Copyright 1977.

The remaining thirteen chapters consist of material that I have compiled and written, and that has not previously been published.

Among those who have provided me with valuable information are the following: Mr. and Mrs. George R. Cartwright, Mr. and Mrs. Franklin B. Tuttle, Mr. Gordon W. Cox, Mr. and Mrs. Donald MacDonald.

I am also grateful to my son, Robert, who corrected my writing and prepared my manuscript for editing.

—H.A. von Behr